Baedeker

D1385997

Gran
Canaria

SIGHTSEEING HIGHLIGHTS ★ ★

Gran Canaria has lots to offer: unique natural landscape with a great variety of flora, sensational hiking, picturesque villages with typical Canarian architecture and not least the bustling island capital Las Palmas. Read on to see what you definitely should not miss!

1 ★★ Gáldar
Remains left by the Guanches, the original inhabitants, make this town a worthwhile destination. ► page 144

2 ★★ Cenobio de Valerón
The function of this cave complex carved in tuff stone is still an enigma. ► page 137

1 Gáldar

2 Cenobio de Valerón

3 Las Palmas

4 Teror

5 Jardín Canario

7 Artenara

6 Caldera de Bandama

©Baedeker

8 Roque Nublo

9 Pozo de las Nieves

11 Playa de Güigüí

10 Barranco de Guayadeque

13 Puerto de Mogán

12 Palmitos Park

14 Dunas/ Playa deMaspalomas

Puerto de Mogán
A popular venue in south Gran Canaria

Palmitos Park
Parrots are the stars of the show here

BAEDEKER'S BEST TIPS

Of all the Baedeker Tips in this guidebook, here is a selection of the best. Experience and enjoy Gran Canaria at its most beautiful!

⚠ On the trail of the Guanches
Excavations, museums and a theme park present the mysterious culture of the early inhabitants of the Canaries. ▸ **page 38**

⚠ Island hopping
For first-time visitors to the Canaries, a trip including two or three islands is ideal.
▸ **page 61**

⚠ Water sports with a difference
How about a banana boat ride, jet skis or paragliding over the water? ▸ **page 96**

⚠ Rural holidays
»Turismo rural« is a good alternative to the usual holiday. We reveal the best addresses. ▸ **page 127**

⚠ Christmas spirit
Beautiful nativity scenes are displayed in Ingenio during the Christmas season.
▸ **page 149**

⚠ Harbour tour
See the town from the water: the *Bahia Cat* tours Puerto de la Luz regularly.
▸ **page 151**

⚠ Sailing Canary-style
In the summer there are Vela Latina regattas in Las Palmas every weekend. You don't have to take part to enjoy them; just watching is fun. ▸ **page 158**

Exuberant ...
... and colourful is the best description of carnival in Las Palmas

⚠ Carnival in Las Palmas
Carnival on the Canaries is by no means the poor cousin of carnival in Rio.
▸ **page 73**

Enigmatic ...
remains of Guanche culture

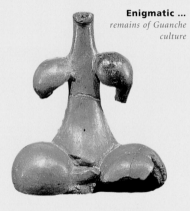

🄷 Colourful folklore
A show especially for tourists, but the graceful dancers in colourful native dress in the folklore show at Pueblo Canario are beautiful. ► page 160

🄷 Casa de Los Músicos
The well-known pianist and conductor Justus Frantz has made himself a small paradise in the hinterland of Maspalomas, where he also rents rooms. ► page 174

🄷 Excursion into the interior
Probably the most beautiful route on Gran Canaria begins about a mile above Mogán ... ► page 176

🄷 Sightseeing on a mini-train
Not just for children: a miniature Western train runs regularly through Playa del Inglés. ► page 180

🄷 Thalasso spa
The largest spa on the island is in San Agustin, where everything revolves around relaxation and recuperation. ► page 197

🄷 Gran Canaria from the air
Whether the view is of magnificent dunes or jagged mountain ranges – a helicopter ride is simply grand. ► page 198

🄷 Fun in the mud
The greatest fun fest on the island is held in San Nicolás de Tolentino, where the whole village takes a mud bath. ► page 199

🄷 Don't miss it!
Queso de flor, »flower cheese« from Santa Maria de Guía, has a unique taste. ► page 203

🄷 Sweet things
Tejeda is a popular stop for those with a sweet tooth. Try the pan de batatas! ► page 207

Aromatic ...
and very tasty: queso de flor from Guía

Colourful ...
... folklore shows in the »Canarian village«

*Sunset over the dunes of
Maspalomas*
▶ page 169

BACKGROUND

Price categories

Hotel (double room)
Luxury: from €140
Mid-range: from €90
Budget: below €90

***Restaurants
(main dish without drinks)***
Expensive: from €20
Moderate: €12 – 20
Inexpensive: under €12

PRACTICALITIES

Artistic wooden balconies decorate the houses of Teror
► page 210

TOURS

SIGHTS FROM A to Z

Background

GRAN CANARIA IS A TOP SPOT
FOR SUN LOVERS WITH
ATTRACTIVE BEACHES OF FINE-
GRAINED SAND – HERE A VIEW OF PLAYA
DE LAS CANTERAS AT LAS PALMAS. YET THE
ISLAND'S INTERIOR OFFERS SURPRISINGLY
UNTOUCHED NATURAL SETTINGS.

SUN, SAND AND MORE ...

A flight of four hours and then the sun shines ... This is why many sun-starved Europeans choose Gran Canaria as their vacation destination year after year. There is no winter on the island, just spring-like temperatures all year round.

With a water temperature of 19°C/66°F, December and January is still a good time to swim in the Atlantic. The air temperature fits the bill, too, and stays above 20°C/68°F. Even the summer is not extremely hot, since the temperatures rarely climb over 25°C/77°F. Should the hot calima winds blow over from North Africa, there is still a light breeze on the beach for cooling off. Small wonder that tourism has taken over this Atlantic sun spot.

Smile ...
for the camera in Las Palmas

Fun Around the Clock

Along the Costa Canaria in the south, holiday resorts line up for miles. This is Spain's largest tourist centre, with accommodation available for more than 160,000 visitors – since the numbers vary, no one seems to have counted exactly. Almost the entire coast has been developed and construction continues. Organized holidays with sports, games and fun around the clock are available here. The miles of beach bordered by a broad belt of golden yellow dunes compensate for many an architectural blemish.

The Green Interior

However, the island doesn't consist of beaches alone. Just a few miles beyond the holiday resorts, the other Gran Canaria begins. Exploring the interior – best with a rental car –soon leads into wild and isolated mountains. The higher up you drive into the mountains, the greener it gets. Palm trees sway in the breeze, quiet pine forests alternate with slopes covered in ferns and flowers. There is a unique diversity of plants – at its best in spring of course. Little cottages gleam between the cliffs. In order to get close to nature, leave the car in a mountain village and begin walking, maybe along the »caminos reales«, the old sheep trails. They cover the island like a labyrinth and take walkers to almost untouched areas.

Romantic ...
evening atmosphere in the narrow streets of Agüimes

Magnificent ...
landscape on the west coast

Happy ...
celebrations at numerous fiestas

Sports ...
the wind is right off southern Gran Canaria

Relaxing ...
at the pool – here at Hotel Palm Beach (Maspalomas)

Exciting ...
sunbathing on the beach at Playa del Inglés

Holiday in the Country

In recent years there has been a trend to »turismo rural«, rural tourism. Various small hotels in the interior or in places off the tourist path have opened up in the past ten years. A stay in a pretty finca or a cottage promises a unique holiday. Rundown farmhouses in remote regions have been restored and are now available as comfortable holiday homes with fragrant pine woods right outside, where tourists can enjoy the peace and quiet.

Canarian Lifestyle

If isolation and untouched nature gets to be too much, you might need a change of pace. The island capital Las Palmas is cosmopolitan without being touristy – even though it has a wonderful long and very clean sandy beach. The old port and trading city with its broad boulevards, narrow streets in the old quarter Vegueta, exclusive villas and exotic parks has typical Canarian atmosphere. Diverse cuisine reflects the colourful variety in the population. Of course, there is entertainment and nightlife as well: around Parque Santa Catalina you can while the night away in countless music clubs, discos and bars.

Despite mass tourism on Gran Canaria, the »island of the blessed« as Plutarch called it, there is still a bit of paradise to discover here. Thousands of holidaymakers who come back again and again testify to this.

Children ...
on tour in Las Palmas

Facts

Gran Canaria, which it gave the entire Canary archipelago its name, is almost in the middle of the island group. It is the third-largest of the Canary Islands after Tenerife and Fuerteventura and is extremely popular among visitors from western and northern Europe.

Nature

The Canary Islands (**Islas Canarias**) are a group of seven larger and six smaller islands in the Atlantic, about 100–300km (60–180mi) from the north-west coast of Africa (Morocco/Western Sahara) and about 1,300km/800mi from Cádiz on the Spanish mainland. The entire archipelago extends 500km/300mi from east to west and 200km/120mi from north to south. Geographically the islands are part of Africa, but politically and socially they are definitely European.

Canary Islands

Until the end of the 20th century there were varied theories on the origin of the Canary Islands. Some thought they were part of the sunken continent **Atlantis**, others believed that the Canary Islands were once part of Africa. The present theory is that the Canaries are elevations of the 4,000m/13,000ft-deep floor of the Atlantic, which is between 150 and 180 million years old here. Tectonic forces from the collision of the European and Atlantic plates caused the eastward-drifting ocean floor to be broken up and compressed, so that parts of it were pushed upwards like wedges. Magma oozed out along the cracks from the Middle Tertiary Period (c30–40 million years ago). In 1999 an expedition with the research ship *Meteor* eliminated any remaining doubts about the volcanic origins of the islands. Scientists on board took countless rock samples from the ocean floor at depths up to 2,500m/8,200ft over a period of weeks. The results showed that all the rocks were of **volcanic origin**. The Canary Islands

Origins of the archipelago

? DID YOU KNOW ...?

■ Pliny (AD 23–79) gave the name of today's Gran Canaria as »Canaria«. He claimed that it derived from the large dogs (Latin »canis«, meaning »dog«) that were thought to live there. While there were already dogs on the Canaries at that time, they were not unusually large. Another explanation refers to the canora bird (from Latin »canere«, »to sing«). The name possibly also comes from Cabo Caunaria (presumably today's Cap Bojador) on the coast of Africa.

did indeed emerge out of the ocean in numerous eruptions and stages of development. The land mass above the surface of the water is only the top of these eruptions. Tenerife and La Gomera probably appeared out of the sea 8–12 million years ago, Fuerteventura 16–20 million years ago and Gran Canaria 13–14 million years ago. The age of La Palma and El Hierro is only 2–3 million years.

There have always been volcanic eruptions on the Canaries. The most recent took place in 1949 and 1971 on La Palma, and in 1909 on Tenerife. In 1730–36 and 1824 large parts of Lanzarote were completely destroyed by eruptions. Gran Canaria and Fuerteventura have

Evidence of volcanoes

← *The landscape near Artenara is beautiful – especially when the almond trees are in blossom in January and February*

Canary Islands Map

not experienced any eruptions in modern times (the last one on Gran Canaria is thought to have been about 3,000 years ago), but these two islands also have volcanic characteristics. Fuerteventura and Lanzarote are marked by moderately high volcanic peaks. Gran Canaria is dominated by former volcanic pipes at the centre of the island; moreover several calderas indicate a volcanic history. The geological term **caldera** refers to a former volcanic crater that was expanded to a cauldron shape by cave-ins and later erosion or by explosions. One possible origin is that during an eruption so much magma was thrown to the surface that a huge hollow formed below. Eventually the surface collapsed and only the edge of the crater remained standing. **Caldera de Bandama** in the north-east of the island is a well-known example of a cauldron-shaped crater on Gran Canaria. **Caldera Pinos de Gáldar** , in the north between Artenara and Valleseco, is believed to be the most recent example of volcanic activity on Gran Canaria. It originated when the peak of the volcano was blown away during an explosion.

Types of rock ► The most common volcanic rock is the bluish-black **basalt**, which can be found in the cliffs between Agaete and Mogán. **Trachyte** is light in colour and has a rough surface, while greyish-green **phonolite** is often used as gravel or for building. **Tuff** is easy to work and thus also often used in building. The ancient Canarians enlarged existing caves in the tuff layers of the barrancos and added new ones. Dark, glassy **obsidian** was named after its discoverer, the Roman Obsidius. The most astonishing characteristic of the light-coloured

Facts and Figures Gran Canaria

Madrid

Canary
Islands

©Baedeker

Population
► 815,000 (total Canaries: 2.1 million)
► between 2006 and 2007 the population
  increased about 1%.
► population density: 522 people per
  sq km/1,333 per sq mile (by
  comparison: Tenerife 389 people per
  sq km/1,007 people per sq mi)

Language
► Spanish (Castellano)

Religion
► 98.3% Roman Catholic

Capital
► Las Palmas de Gran Canaria

Administration
► Spanish province Las Palmas de Gran
  Canaria, part of the Autonomous
  Region of the Canary Islands (Comuni-
  dad Autonóma de Canarias)
► highest political authority: Cabildo
  Insular (island council)

Economy
► tourism is the most important source of
  income.
► main export products: bananas and
  tomatoes

Island group
► Canary Islands
  (Islas Canarias in Spanish)
► major islands: Gran Canaria, Lanzarote,
  Fuerteventura, Tenerife, La Palma, La
  Gomera and El Hierro

Location
► between 27° 92' and 28° 45' north and
  between 13° 90' and 14° 31' west

Distances
► to the African mainland:
  300km/180mi
► to Spain: 1,300km/780mi

Area
► 1,532 sq km/591 sq mi (all Canary
  Islands: 7,541sq km/2,912 sq mi)
► this makes Gran Canaria the third-
  largest island in the archipelago

Size
► length and width: approx. 50km/30mi
► length of coastline:
  approx. 240km/140mi
► highest elevation:
  Pozo de las Nieves 1,949m/6,394ft

Tourism
► approx. 2.8 million foreign guests every
  year
► about 30% come from Great Britain
  and another 30% from Germany
► of all tourists who visit Spain, 31% visit
  the Canaries (35% the Balearic Islands)
► most important tourist centres: Maspalomas, Playa del Inglés, Puerto de
  Mogán and Puerto Rico
► hotel beds: 160,000

pumice is that it floats. It is actually a rock foam made of gaseous, thickening lava. It holds water well and is thus used on the Canaries for dry farming.

Landscape   Gran Canaria, with a diameter of about 50km/30mi and a circumference of about 240km/140mi, is almost completely circular. After Tenerife and Fuerteventura it is the third-largest island of the Canaries. The centre of Gran Canaria consists of a mountain range. The highest peak is **Pozo de las Nieves** (1,949m/6,394ft), which is surrounded by several peaks that are almost the same height and there-

Sunset at Roque Nublo with a view of Mount Teide on Tenerife

fore less dominant than Teide on Tenerife. Bizarre rocks like the **Roque Nublo** (1,813m/5,948ft) are characteristic of Gran Canaria. These are the remains of extensive rock coverings. While the surrounding rock was eroded away, the harder parts, which were originally volcanic pipes, remained.

The central mountain range, also called the **Cumbre**, divides the island into two completely different types of landscape. While the northern slopes are covered with lush vegetation, the south is more like a desert, except for some fertile valleys. Deep valleys (**barrancos**) radiate from the Cumbre to the coasts. The largest canyons are in the west and south of Gran Canaria; the barrancos of Agaete, Aldea, Mogán and Fataga are especially impressive.

The mountains fall steeply in cliffs to the coast in the west; in the north they gradually turn into hills bordered by cliffs and a surf coast. The only sand or pebble beaches are at the mouths of barrancos. In the east and south coastal plains with some large beaches border the mountains. The most beautiful and longest **beaches** are near Maspalomas/Playa del Inglés. The extensive beaches and dunes were once attributed to frequent sandstorms from Africa, but since the sand is mainly made of carbonates it can only have originated in the coastal shelf. As the land became elevated, sand terraces of various heights were formed.

There are no perennial rivers on Gran Canaria, but some springs, including those near Firgas and Los Berrazales in Barranco de Agaete, are very productive.

Plants and Animals

Canary Islands flora is unique for two reasons. On the one hand, plants from almost every zone of vegetation on earth exist in a relatively limited area; on the other hand, there is an unusually **large percentage of endemic plants**, i.e. plants that exist only here. Canarian flora includes almost 3,000 different species, many of which were introduced as agricultural and decorative plants. It is estimated that about 1,300 species of plants on the island already existed in pre-historic times. Of these 30% are endemic. | **Diverse flora**

Many fossils of fruits and leaves that have been found in the Mediterranean region, in the Alps and in southern Russia prove that plants that only grow on the Canary Islands today were once common over larger areas. Climatic changes at the end of the present Tertiary period (beginning of the ice age, drying out of the Sahara) forced plants out of their earlier territories, but they were able to survive on the isolated Canary Islands. Moreover extreme differences in elevation on the western Canaries and on Gran Canaria made it possible for the plants to survive by migrating to different altitudes.

The varying elevation and trade winds caused the different zones of vegetation on the Canaries. | **Vegetation zones**

ISLAND OF CONTRASTS

Gran Canaria's south offers sunshine galore and endless beaches, but the scenery in the often cloudy north is completely different: lush greenery everywhere. The spectacular interior features strangely shaped mountains and pretty villages.

① Pinar de Tamadaba

Open pine forest covers the 1,444m/4,738ft-high Tamadaba. The pine trees are vital to the island's water supply since they cause the water in the clouds to condense.

② Embalse Caidero de la Niña

This reservoir was built in the mid-20th century in the interior to relieve Gran Canaria's constant water shortage. Today the emphasis is on desalination plants.

③ Caldera de Bandama

The crater cauldron is visible evidence of the island's volcanic past. It was made about 5,000 years ago in a violent explosion.

④ Roque Nublo

»Cloud rock« is a striking pinnacle, the remains of a former volcanic pipe.

⑤ Pozo de las Nieves

Pozo or Pico de las Nieves with 1,949m/6,394ft is the highest mountain on the island. Despite the name (»snow fountain«), snow hardly ever lies here.

⑥ Barranco de Fataga

From the centre of the island, deep gorges like the Barranco de Fataga fan out to the coast. The floors of the narrow valleys are used for agriculture.

⑦ Dunas de Maspalomas

Nowhere else on the Canary Islands are the sand dunes as extensive as here. They were created several thousand years ago during the last glacial period. At that time sea level was up to 90m/300ft lower than it is now.

Just like the western Canaries, the north of Gran Canaria is lush and green, with many a small paradise to discover

Barranco de Agaete is considered one of the most beautiful barrancos on the island. Local people just call it »El Valle«

Potatoes, grain and corn are grown on terraced fields at higher elevations

© Baedeker

Cruz de Tejeda marks the highest pass on the island (1,490m/4,888ft)

A touch of the Sahara: the dunes at Maspalomas

The lowest level is dry as a desert. Along with succulents like Canary Island spurge, the Canarian date palm grows here. In the south this zone has an elevation of up to 1,000m/3,300ft, while in the north it is restricted to the coast. Here the natural vegetation between 200m/650ft and 600m/2,000ft includes varieties of juniper and dragon trees; laurel trees appear above 600m/2,000ft. The deciduous zone, which is always green, borders the fayal-brezal formation (faya = bog myrtle; brezo = tree heath) at an altitude of 1,100m/3,600ft. Tree heath grows up to 15m/50ft high, but can also develop into a shrub or dwarf shrub. Together with the laurel zone, the fayal-brezal heathland is also called »Monte Verde«. In the northern half of the western Canaries the pine forest zone begins at 1,500m/5,000ft; in the southern half Canary pine already grows at 1,000m/3,300ft.

Dragon tree The unique and most characteristic plant of the Canaries is the dragon tree (Dracaena draco). It is a member of the **Ruscaceae family**, and with its tall trunk and branched crown is a close relative of the yucca. Dragon trees grow relatively quickly: in 50 years they can attain a height of 4–5m/13–16ft. A few old specimens are even up to 20m/65ft high. The ends of dragon tree branches form a bunch of dark green, long, sword-like leaves. Since the dragon tree only forms branches after about ten years, when it first blossoms, the young ones bear no resemblance to the old trees. As they have no annual rings, the age can only be determined by the number of branches, but the branches grow at irregular intervals. Dragon trees had a special meaning for the early Canarians, who used the »dragon's blood«, the sap that oozed from the trunk and turned red on exposure to air, as an ointment.

Canary date palm The Canary date palm (Phoenix canariensis) has spread from the islands into the entire Mediterranean region. It is closely related to the North African and Arab date palm, but its trunk is shorter and its crown fuller and more decorative with larger fans. However, its fruits are woody and not edible. Beautiful examples of Phoenix canariensis can be seen in southern Gran Canaria, especially in Barranco de Fataga.

Canary pine The long, flexible needles of the Canary pine (Pinus canariensis) always grow in groups of three. The hard reddish wood was and

The island of »eternal spring« lives up to its reputation: flowering plants at Roque Nublo in the central mountains

still is used for panelled ceilings and balconies. The pines (in Spanish »tea«) grow at an elevation of 1,000–2,000m/3,300–6,600ft and are able to condense water out of the passing clouds. It drips from their needles like rain. This filtered water not only irrigates the trees but is also an important part of the island's **water supply**.

Even though the forests of the Canaries have been decimated over the course of centuries, some laurel forest remains on Gran Canaria. The most accessible area is in the north of the island at Moya (**Los Tilos**). Canary laurel (Laurus canariensis), like the Canary pine, also contributes to the island's water supply. It is usually around 8–10m/

Canary laurel

27–33ft high, but can reach 20m/66ft; its dark green leaves, which can be used as bay leaf, are pointed and elliptical. Los Tilos forest has about 15 different varieties of laurel, but all look very similar: it takes some effort to distinguish them by their leaves and bark.

Crassula

Crassulacaea are succulent plants that can grow in arid places. They store water for dry periods; rosette leaves reduce evaporation. On the Canary Islands there are more than 80 varieties of Crassulacaea, which remain green and can get to be very old.

Canary spurge

Canary spurge prefers dry mountain slopes and rocks. It is called »**cardón**« on the Canaries. At first glance this native of the Canaries looks like a cactus, but it differs from cacti in the poisonous milky sap in its branches, roots and fruit and in its inconspicuous leaves. Canary spurge grows slowly. The giant ones that can be seen in the southern part of the island may be hundreds of years old.

Prickly pear

Another typical succulent is the **prickly pear** (Opuntia ficus indica). It was introduced to the Canaries in the 16th century and often covers the slopes of the island up to the middle elevations. Its edible fruit is sold on the island. Cochineals (scale insects) are grown on prickly pears and processed for their red dye. This industry is now significant only on Lanzarote.

Decorative plants

Along with the prickly pear and a few varieties of agave, the Spanish conquerors brought several varieties of luxuriously blooming plants to the islands. Oleander, hibiscus and of course bougainvillea abound in the parks and gardens. In the winter months **poinsettias** blossom red in many places on Gran Canaria. These dense bushes can grow to be 3–4m/10–13ft high. The **bird of paradise** or **strelitzia** with its unique flowers looks very exotic.

Cultivated plants

The cultivation of various food plants also changed the original island vegetation. The lower and middle elevations are now covered with banana plants, fruit trees, vegetables and vineyards.

Banana

By far the **most important cultivated plant** is the banana. The variety that has been cultivated on the Canaries since the late 19th century, Musa cavendishii, is small and resistant to weather; it was imported from Indochina. The trunk of the banana plant consists of a number of long, stiff and juicy leaf shafts. At the end of the shaft is a long, fibrous leaf. When the plant is about one year old the flower forms, with the female part at the bottom and the male part at the top. Depending on how much sunlight it gets and the altitude (bananas flourish on the Canaries at elevations up to 300–400m/ 1,000–1,300ft) the bananas ripen in 4–6 months. A bunch of bananas weighs on average 25–30kg/55–66lb, sometimes even up to 60kg/ 130lb. The plants die after the bananas ripen, but in the mean time have formed offspring. Of these the strongest survives and matures, and will itself flower after a year.

Fauna

The fauna of Gran Canaria is far less extensive than the flora, but again there is a relatively large number of endemic species. Of the 328 species that are protected in Spain, 63 live on the Canaries.

Mammals

Apart from rabbits, hedgehogs and bats there are no endemic large mammals.

Reptiles

It is reassuring to know that neither scorpions nor poisonous snakes inhabit the islands. **Lizards** can be seen everywhere, as well as the occasional slow worm, a legless lizard. The largest lizard is the 80cm/ 30in Lacerta stehlinii, which is endemic to Gran Canaria.

Birds

There is great diversity in the birds on the island. Blackbirds, blue tits, a type of robin, chaffinches, woodpeckers, various kinds of pigeons, buzzards, kestrels as well as seagulls and ibis live here. Occasionally the song of the capirote, the Canary nightingale, can be heard. But anyone looking for the yellow **canary** songbird outdoors will be disappointed. There is only an inconspicuous variety, the Canary serin (see Baedeker Special p.26).

Insects

Gran Canaria is home to a very large number of endemic insects. Butterfly fans are in their element. The Canary admiral as well as the brimstone butterfly with orange front wings stand out. The largest variety is the monarch, which can have a wingspan of up to 10cm/ 4in.

Marine life

The waters around the Canary Islands teem with fish. Salmon, tuna, squid, moray eel, bass, skate and sprat are among them. Mullet is caught around the islands and many menus include vieja, a variety of mullet that only lives in these waters. The rocky coastal areas are the territory of conger eels. Dangerous sharks have never been seen along the coast, but **swarms of dolphins** and **whales** accompany the ferries. Almost 20 different kinds of whales have been sighted off the coasts of the Canaries, including some endangered ones. Pilot

? DID YOU KNOW …?

■ Whale watching around the islands has increased dramatically in the last ten years. Many boats recklessly get too close to the whales, which can alarm them. The fast ferries that run between Gran Canaria and Tenerife also endanger the whales: accidents happen regularly since the whales cannot manoeuvre fast enough to get out of the way.

CANARY BIRDS

Don't go looking for the yellow songbirds in their natural habitat. The ancestor of the domestic canary is the inconspicuous European serin (Serinus canaria).

It has grey-green feathers and doesn't sing nearly as nicely as its domestic cousin. The birds generally live in large flocks, mainly on Gran Canaria and the western Canary Islands. When Spanish invaders penetrated the interior of the Canary Islands in the 15th century, they found that the local people kept these birds in small cages. The Spanish conquerors, conscious of their value, took the birds back home as part of the spoils of war. The Portuguese had already brought canaries from Madeira and the Azores to Europe in the early 15th century.

Spanish monks were the first to breed the birds. Astute businessmen, they sold only the males, thus securing the trade monopoly for themselves and keeping it for almost a century.

Symbol of Wealth

In these times only the nobility and wealthy commoners could afford to buy a canary. The little warblers soon became a **symbol of wealth** – in Italy, France and England as well as in Spain. The monks' lucrative monopoly ended in the mid-16th century, for reasons that are open to specula-

No pretty little canaries like these live in the wild on Gran Canaria. There is only a plainer, wild variety here

tion. Some say that a trading ship en route to Livorno sank off the coast of Elba. The male canaries on board got away, and some mated on the mainland with the southern European serin (Serinus serinus), close relatives of theirs. Their young »were caught and bred«. But it is more likely that among the many males that were sold, an occasional female slipped through, as only an experienced breeder can tell the sex of a canary with certainty.

Coal Mines and a Football Club

In the 17th century the canary soon became the common man's pet in many parts of Europe. At that time many people in the Tyrol region of the Alps were miners; by raising and selling canaries they were able to supplement their income. Canaries not only helped support the family, but were taken into the mines to serve as a living alarm system. If a canary died suddenly in its cage, it usually meant that the poisonous, but colourless and odourless gas carbon monoxide was present. The miners then had little time to leave their tunnels

and seek safety. The birds saved lives, a service they performed in coal pits and other mines around the world well into the 20th century. In England the city of Norwich became the centre for breeding canaries, as the birds were brought by Flemish immigrants fleeing from Spanish rule. They became a symbol of the city and gave Norwich City Football Club its nickname.

Popular Pet

Domestic canaries have become popular pets. There are now millions of them all over the world – on the Canary Islands as well, the home of their ancestors and their cousins who still live in the wild.

whales can be seen relatively often; they are recognizable by their round heads. They can be 4–5m/13–16ft long and weigh up to 1.5t.

Nature Protection and Ecology

Environmental factors

The tourist boom and the construction that went along with it penetrated deeply the habitat of native flora. Many endemic species are threatened with extinction. In the **Jardín Canario** near Tafira the endangered species are grown so that they can be transferred to their natural habitat.

The deforestation that has taken place since the Spanish conquest and increased since the end of the 19th century has had devastating effects on the ecology. Large areas were deforested in order to increase agriculture. Thus on Gran Canaria less than 1% of the original renowned laurel forests remain. In past decades reforestation has been carried out on Gran Canaria, as the forest is essential for the island's water supply and prevents erosion of the mountainsides. At first mainly eucalyptus trees were planted. In recent years pines were used, albeit a fast-growing North American variety (Pinus insignis) instead of the local Pinus canariensis.

Ecological problems of tourism

Air pollution on the Canaries is pleasantly moderate due to the warm climate, the almost constant wind and the lack of heating. Ecological problems derive mainly from the increase in tourism, which caused countless hotel complexes to be built from the 1970s and whole sections of the island to be covered in concrete. This uninhibited **building mania** can be seen in southern Gran Canaria, in Playa del Inglés, Maspalomas, Puerto Rico and other developed areas. While fewer building permits are now given for tourist facilities – in the past years the emphasis has been on quality tourism and improving infrastructure – there remain many projects that have been approved but not yet begun. Untouched sections of coastline will continue to be sacrificed for tourism. For example, at Playa de Veneguera it is intended to add another 20,000 beds in the near future. Along with building over the land, mass tourism also makes problems in the disposal of refuse, water supply and treatment of waste water.

Lack of water

Fresh water is not plentiful on the Canaries. The population has grown in recent years and consumes more water. The thousands of tourists do not want to do without their daily shower: they use more than twice as much water per day as the local people. In the past reservoirs such as Presa de Soria holding up to 40 million cubic metres/ 10.5 billion gallons ensured the water supply to tourist centres in the south, but at present they are often empty. Thus the groundwater has increasingly been tapped. On Gran Canaria water is pumped from wells that usually have a diameter of 3m/10ft and are 150–200m/500–660ft deep, some even up to 300m/1,000ft. As a result the water table has fallen in the past 25 years by 100m/330ft.

Maspalomas: holiday flats as far as the eye can see

Half of the more than 2,000 wells and springs have dried up. Moreover, the further the water table sinks, the more seawater seeps in. This precarious situation has been alleviated somewhat in recent years through the building of **desalination plants**. The first was started in 1965 on Lanzarote. Today this island gets almost 100% of its water from the ocean. On Gran Canaria there are presently more than 100 small and large desalination plants; more than half of the island's water supply comes from the Atlantic. The desalination technology works well, but the problem is that the plants all run on fossil fuels, i.e. petroleum.

Nature protection was an unknown concept on the Canary Islands for a long time. However, things have changed since the 1990s. A visible sign is the lagoon at Maspalomas (Charca de Maspalomas). An almost finished hotel was torn down here and an area of 328ha/ 810 acres placed under protection. A law on the protection of nature covering compensation, government acquisition of nature zones and stricter measures against ecological crimes now applies.

In 1994 the Canary Islands parliament **established a national park** 20,000ha/49,400 acres in size in the centre of the island around Roque Nublo. As building permits are no longer given for this area and agriculture is no longer allowed here, there is a lot of public opposition to this project, and little progress has been made on the park.

Nature protection

Climate

Eternal spring

The Canary Islands have a warm temperate climate that justifies the phrase »eternal spring«. The climate is milder and more pleasant than one would expect in these latitudes. It is influenced mainly by **trade winds**, but also by the **high pressure areas off the Azores** and the cool **Canaries current**.

In general, the weather can change quickly on the Canaries. There are no long periods of bad weather. If the sun ever hides behind clouds, just drive a short distance further and it will be shining again.

Pleasant temperatures

The temperature varies remarkably little during the course of the year. The average winter temperature is around 19°C/66°F, while the summers rarely get above 24°C/75°F (►Practicalities, When to Go). In mountainous areas the temperatures are lower at higher elevations and tend to vary more during the course of the year. The influence of the Sahara on the climate is also noticeable at times: when the hot dry **calima** blows across from North Africa, mainly in July and August, the thermometer can suddenly rise about 10°C/18°F. Sometimes the fine sand and dust in the air reduces visibility to only about 100m/100yd. The heat wave generally only lasts for three to four days. Water temperatures in the winter are around 19°C/66°F, in the summer around 22°C/71°F.

Trade Winds

westerly flow

Tropic of Cancer

north-east trade wind

easterly flow

Equator (ITC)

easterly flow

south-east trade wind

Tropic of Capricorn

westerly flow

© Baedeker (according to Flohn)

Rainfall is generally limited to the winter months. It is caused by cyclones from northern latitudes. No rain has fallen on Fuerteventura and Lanzarote for years, and southern Gran Canaria no longer has much rain in the winter either. The northern coast gets about 500mm/20in of rain, the mid-range mountains about 600–800mm/25–30in annually, the higher elevations less. The **lowest altitude for snowfall** lies at about 1,200m/4,000ft, but generally snow lies only on the almost 2,000m/6,600ft-high Pozo or Pico de las Nieves for a short time in the winter.

Clouds form regularly over Gran Canaria and the western Canaries at the middle elevations in the early mornings, but disappear again towards evening. The clouds rarely bring rain, but they do cause precipitation in the form of fog and dew. The clouds occur almost all year and are caused by **trade winds** from the northeast that blow at up to force 4.

Unlike other climatic influences, the trade wind is consistent. It begins at the equator, where the sun warms the surface of the earth the most (inner tropic convergence, ITC). The warm air rises, then cools and moves at an altitude of 12–15km/ 7–9mi towards the poles. After cooling some more it sinks to the earth's surface at about 30° north and then flows back to the equator. However, the rotation of the earth diverts the wind streams from their course. In the northern hemisphere a north-east wind results; in the southern hemisphere its direction is south-east. Above 1,500m/5,000ft they are warm dry winds, and below that they are cooler and moister. As long as the upper and lower layers persist (**enversion**), hardly any clouds form, but if the flow runs into a mountain, the inversion is disrupted. The cooler, damper lower wind streams against the sunny warm mountain slopes, is warmed and begins to rise. Then it cools down again and the moisture condenses. **Clouds** form between 600m and 1,700m (2,000ft and 5,600ft), though not at night because of the cooler air. Since the winds blow from the north-east, clouds do not form in the south. Only warm, dry downdraughts occur there. The influence of the trade winds is reduced in the winter. The sun's rays strike the northern hemisphere at a much more acute angle, which causes the zone of trade winds to move southwards and the Canary Islands to be influenced by Atlantic low pressure systems at times.

Since the island is so close to the equator, the number of daylight hours does not vary as much between summer and winter on Gran Canaria as in northern Europe: the longest summer day has about 14 hours of daylight, the shortest winter day about 11 hours. **Twilight** is very short.

Daylight hours

Population · Economy

The Autonomous Region of the Canary Islands has a population of about 1.9 million people; of these 790,000 live on Gran Canaria, which makes the island the most densely populated of the archipelago by far. There are about 515 people per sq km (1,333 per sq mi), while on Tenerife, the largest of the Canary Islands, the population density is only 389 per sq km (1,007 per sq mi; the corresponding figure for England is 392 per sq km or 1,015 per sq mi). The population of Gran Canaria increased dramatically in the 20th century, from only about 130,000 around 1900 to 330,000 by 1950 and 630,000 at the beginning of the 1980s. The largest urban area is Las Palmas de Gran Canaria; almost half of the island population lives in the capital city.

Statistics

Due to unemployment many Canarians had to emigrate in the past. South America was the destination of choice. Today about 300,000 Canarians are said to be living in Caracas (Venezuela). In the meantime the South American countries accept few immigrants, which is causing the population to grow again.

Anthropologists have proven that the Canarian people are different from mainland Spaniards. Many characteristics show that they are **descendants of the original inhabitants of the islands**.

The families have a **patriarchal structure**. The man is the head of the family; the woman takes care of the household and the children. As a result of the high rate of unemployment and low salaries (the average Canarian salary is about 1250 euros per month), and due to the relatively high cost of living, the women are often forced to find some work to supplement the family income. Even though small families dominate in the cities, extended families often live together in rural areas. The number of children is declining, however.

Economy

Tourism as »monoculture« In the past three decades there has been a clear economic upswing on the Canary Islands. The average income on the islands is now higher than in many parts of Spain and amounts to 82% of the EU average. But since the economy is completely dependent on tourism, the reduction in the number of visitors in the past years has caused serious economic problems. The service sector makes up 79% of the regional economy, and more than 70% of employed persons work in the tourist industry.

Agricultural change Over the centuries the agricultural export products have changed. The orchilla lichen, which flourished on Lanzarote and Fuerteventura, was valued in ancient times because it was used to make red or violet dye, giving the two eastern Canary Islands the name Purpuraria. After the Spanish conquest **sugar cane** was cultivated. However, this branch of the economy died out as early as the 16th century due to the competition from Central America. Then the main product was **wine**. In the 17th and 18th centuries, rich Canarian Malmsey wine was in great demand at European courts. But tastes changed; imported disease (mildew in 1852 and 1878) put an end to this branch of the economy. In the 19th century **cochineal** was raised. This cactus parasite, which is used to make a red dye, flourished on the fields of prickly pears, but lost its importance when aniline dyes were developed. At present cochineal is only used in lipsticks and to

Gran Canarians celebrate festivals enthusiastically –
here at the Bajada de la Rama in Agaete

colour cordials, soft drinks and candy. The industry continues on a small scale on Lanzarote. At that time the **banana** saved the economy, when a small robust variety (Musa cavendishii) was imported from Indochina. Already in 1890 it was being cultivated on a large scale on Gran Canaria and the western Canaries. However, this branch of the economy too has faced problems for decades. Since the small but very tasty banana looks almost pitiful compared to the Central and South American competition, it is almost impossible to sell it in Europe. Moreover, production costs are much higher than in other countries. Even though production was subsidized by the Spanish government and the EU, it was no longer profitable for many farmers. When the EU subsidies cease, as is planned, many farmers will have to look for other ways to make a living.

Banana plant

Banana cultivation is concentrated in the northern half of Gran Canaria. The delicious fruit flourishes at elevations up to 400m/1,300ft. Higher up the main crops are potatoes, grain, maize, sugar cane (especially around Arucas), cabbage, figs and other produce. In the south and south-west **tomatoes** are the most important products. Gran Canaria is the largest Canarian producer of tomatoes for the European market. The tomatoes produced from November to May are exported. They are covered with plastic sheeting to protect them from the wind. Although exports have been increasing for years, the Canarian farmers hardly profit. A tomato plant needs three litres of water a day, which makes production expensive due to the high cost of water on Gran Canaria. The production costs for a kilo of tomatoes are more than twice that of Morocco, for example.

Winegrowing on Gran Canaria is insignificant; there are only a few hundred hectares left around Tafira. The agricultural products most likely to bring a profit are the more exotic ones like mangos, papayas, avocados, or cut flowers.

Livestock plays a secondary role. Beef and pork production only covers part of local needs. Telde is the centre of cattle-raising on Gran Canaria, but the cattle are generally kept in pens since they could injure themselves on the uneven terrain.

Fishing

Traditional Canarian fishing has been declining since 2000 at the latest. At that time the negotiations on catch quotas and territories between the European Union and Morocco failed. From 72,000t in 1999 the catch fell to 8,400t in 2003. At the same time **fish farming** along the coast increased about 550%. Much of the fish consumed on the island has been imported for decades already.

Industry

Industry produces about 17% of the gross regional product, but the high costs of importing raw materials and of energy continue to limit the development of this branch of the economy. A few smaller or mid-sized industries process foods, while others process wood and make paper and cardboard, building materials or fertilizer. Small businesses produce crafts such as embroidered articles.

Trade

The Canary Islands have been a **free trade zone** since 1852. This caused trade to boom. The lack of water, raw materials and energy, however, made economic development difficult. Thus the balance of trade has been negative for a long time. Imports are increasing, especially from the Spanish motherland. Important imports are crude oil, consumer products and food, as well as mechanical and electrical machines and vehicles. Exports are mainly agrarian.

Energy

The growing need for energy (between 1992 and 2002 it grew 73% on the Canaries) is met mainly with **oil**. Alternative forms of energy are only used privately or on an experimental level. Solar energy is used on a small scale for desalinating seawater. **Wind energy** is also used. The dry warm winds blow across the islands at an average speed of 40 km/h (24mph). One of the most important wind power facilities is in Barranco de Tirajana on the southern coast of Gran Canaria. 67 wind generators here produce 20 megawatts of electricity.

Tourism

The first tourists, mainly English and Scandinavians, came to Gran Canaria in the 1950s. They either went to Las Palmas or the Parador at Cruz de Tejeda. Around 1960 there were only 2,500 hotel beds on the island. In the late 1960s and early 1970s the building of the hotel city Maspalomas/Playa del Inglés drastically increased the number of visitors. The 1970s and 1980s saw a real boom in tourism. In the 1990s growth was interrupted more than once, but the trend continued upwards. In the record years of 1999 and 2000 about 10 million visitors came to the Canary Islands. The numbers have stagnated since 2001 and begun to drop. In recent years about 2.8 million foreign tourists came to Gran Canaria every year.

History

When were the Canary Islands first settled? Who were the Guanches? What happened to them after the Spanish conquest of the islands? Research has found answers to these questions.

Mythology

Hardly any other place on earth has been so shrouded in myth as the Canary Islands since the beginning of their history. Elysian Fields, Happy Isles, Islands of the Blessed, Gardens of the Hesperides and so on were the names used by ancient authors such as Homer, Hesiod, Plato, Strabo, Virgil, Horace, Ptolemy and Plutarch for islands at the western edge of the world which were supposed to be like paradise on earth. In the Middle Ages travellers, poets and scholars such as Isidore of Seville enthused about flowering islands in the distant west.

Happy Isles

Ancient Inhabitants

From 500 BC	Settlement in several waves of immigration
14th–15th centuries	Simple herding and farming culture

Dated archaeological finds show that the Canaries were first settled after 500 BC. Scientists now agree that the roots of the ancient Canarians go back to the Berber culture of **North Africa**. Examination of skeletons has shown that the ancient Canarians and North Africans are related. There are also similarities to the Berber cultures; comparisons of language fragments as found in indigenous place names, in documents and inscriptions (petroglyphs) have also been fruitful. It is now assumed that the immigration from Africa to the Canaries took place in several waves, but it is still not clear why these people left their North African home. Possible causes are the growing desertification of the Sahara region and the oppression of the Roman occupation. There is also only speculation as to how the immigrants got to the islands. As no remains of boats have been found, it is assumed that reed boats were used which decayed later.

Berbers settle on the islands

> **? DID YOU KNOW ...?**
>
> ■ The name »Guanche« is often used for all the ancient peoples of the Canary Islands. However, this expression was originally applied only to the residents of Tenerife. The word »Guanche« comes from the ancient Canarian language and means »son of Tenerife«.

When the Europeans conquered the Canaries in the 14th and 15th centuries they found a simple **herding and farming culture** which

Guanche life and culture

← *The most important early Canarian find: the idol of Tara, which was discovered on Gran Canaria*

seemed to have no contact whatsoever to the rest of the world. The island was divided into two realms, each of which was ruled by a king, a **guanarteme**. The ruler of the western half of the island had his capital in Gáldar; the other ruled the eastern half of Gran Canaria from Telde. The royal succession was passed down the female line, but the culture was not a matriarchy. The ruler was not the woman but her husband, whom she chose and thus legitimized. The female succession is certain to have enhanced the position of women in the society. There is also evidence that women also played a role in religious rites. Little is known about the social structure. There were noblemen and farmers; nobility was not inherited, but awarded on the grounds of personal virtue.

The Guanches raised barley, wheat and pulses on small fields but had no ploughs. They kept goats as domestic livestock. The staple food was **gofio**, roasted barley which was milled and mixed with honey and water, kneaded and rolled into balls. Goat meat, milk and butter were also important parts of the diet. Seafood also played a role.

Most ancient Canarians lived in **caves**. These were especially suited to the climate. The cave interiors were made smooth; often wood ceilings were added. Sometimes artificial caves were made. This could lead to an elaborate system of caves, as seen in Cenobio de Valerón. There are also a few stone structures, especially tombs (e.g. the tumulus of Gáldar) and covered living pits as well as straw-covered clay huts.

The **clothing** of the ancient Canarians must have seemed unusual to the Spanish invaders. The Guanches wore goatskins that were carefully sewn together with plant thorns. Fabric woven from palm and other fibres was also used for clothing. Their **tools and weapons** also appeared primitive to 15th-century Spaniards. The Guanches defended themselves only with wooden clubs and stones that they threw. In hand-to-hand combat they also used thin stone blades which were so sharp that they could be used as cutting tools.

The ancient Canarians believed in an all-powerful supreme being, called »Acoran« (»the greatest, highest«) on Gran Canaria. Holy mountains, as the place where the divine and earthly worlds met, played a major role in religious rituals on the islands. Animal sacrifices and libations were made there.

Mysterious mummies It is remarkable that the world of the dead remained closely bound up with the world of the living. Settlement and funeral sites are not always easily distinguished. Natural and artificial caves served both as

! **Baedeker TIP**

On the trail of the Guanches
No-one interested in the Guanche culture should miss the Museo Canario in Las Palmas. The »cave palace« Cenobio de Valerón, the recently opened Parque Arqueológico de Arteara near Fataga and the excavations at La Guancha also give interesting insights into this ancient culture. A visit to the theme park Mundo Aborigen, a replica of an ancient Canarian village, is also fun.

Mummies in Museo Canario in Las Palmas: after being embalmed the bodies were wrapped in reed mats or leather

residential and as funeral sites. The dead from higher levels of society were mummified. The corpses were rubbed with goat butter and conserved with heat and smoke. The brain was never removed, and the internal organs only in some cases. These techniques of mummification were primitive compared to those of the ancient Egyptians. The mummies were not conserved for long, and the funeral grottoes were clearly used many times. The mummies found there, which can be seen in the Museo Canario in Las Palmas, were not very old.

The little that has remained of the ancient Canarian language is mostly found in place names. **Similarities with the Berber languages** are evident. The islands did not have a unified language; rather different dialects were spoken on each one. Basic expressions like »gofio« and »tamarco« (fur cloak) existed on several islands.

Enigmatic rock inscriptions

When the Spanish conquered the Canaries the local people had no system of writing, but rock inscriptions have been found regularly even in recent times. The first were discovered in 1867 on La Palma (Cueva Belmaco); in 1870 an entire chapter of the history of the writing system was found on El Hierro (Los Letreros): a rock wall was inscribed with both symbols representing ideas and concepts, which the viewer has to interpret, and with signs that come close to modern alphabets. Transitions can be seen between the two writing systems. On Gran Canaria near **Barranco de Balos** (Lomo de los Letreros) spirals and concentric circles were found inscribed into rock (megalithic petroglyphs). Nothing comparable has been found on Tenerife and La Gomera. The inscriptions have not been deciphered and it is doubtful that they ever will be, since souvenir hunters have removed large parts of the rocks. It is also not clear whether the inscriptions were made by the Canarians themselves or were left behind by visitors to the islands.

Conquest and Colonial Period

AD 23–79	The Canarians are mentioned in the *Naturalis Historia* of Pliny.
1312	Lancelotto Malocello lands on Lanzarote.
1478–83	Conquest of Gran Canaria
1479	The treaty of Alcáçovas gives the Canary Islands to Spain.
1492	Christopher Columbus lands on Gran Canaria during his first voyage of discovery.

First contact There has been much discussion on whether or not the **Phoenicians**, who were daring and skilful sailors, landed on the Canaries on their voyages of discovery along the West African coast in the first millennium BC. There is no proof. The first surviving report of a visit to the Canaries is by **Pliny the Elder** (AD 23–79). He described an expedition to the Canaries in his *Naturalis Historia*, which was made for the king of Mauretania, Juba II (d. AD 23). It is not known whether this expedition was a success, but at least the name »Canaria« appears for the first time in Pliny's text. The first clear evidence of a Roman landing on the Canaries comes in the form of 3rd or 4th-century pottery that was found on Lanzarote and La Graciosa. Up to the early 14th century it is likely that seafarers and adventurers occasionally reached the Canaries. These islands at the western edge of the then known world were mentioned many times in European, Byzantine and Arabic sources. However, due to their distance and the fact that there did not appear to be any material gain, the seafaring powers of Europe and the Near East showed no interest in dominating them.

Only in the 14th century did the Canaries get the attention of European seafaring powers. This began with reports of the travels of Lancelotto Malocello from Genoa: Malocello landed in 1312 on the island that was later named after him, Lanzarote, and liked it so much that he stayed there for several years. Many sailors, traders and pirates stopped at the Canary Islands after that. They hoped to get rich quickly by enslaving the indigenous people. Several documents of the second half of the 14th century refer to the wealth of the archipelago in human wares.

Conquest of the Canaries

As the sovereign of »all lands that have not yet been discovered«, in 1344 Pope Clement VI named Luís de la Cerda, a relative of the Spanish royal family, **king of the Canary Islands**, but this title did not include any claim to property. Luís de la Cerda's successor was Roberto de Bracamonte, who was also content with the title and took no steps to take possession of his domain. He left this to his cousin **Jean de Béthencourt** (1359–1425; ► Famous People). Along with the Spanish nobleman **Gadifer de la Salle** (c1340–1422) the Norman Jean de Béthencourt was the first to try to conquer the Canary Islands for the Spanish crown. After the occupation of Lanzarote in 1402, Béthencourt was given the title »king of the Canary Islands«. In the following years he also gained the islands of Fuerteventura and El Hierro. Béthencourt, whose attempts to conquer Gran Canaria and La Palma failed, returned to the European mainland in 1406. He named his nephew Maciot de Béthencourt as viceroy of the islands. At the intervention of the Spanish king, Maciot de Béthencourt had to give back the title due to misrule, but profited from this situation several times: he sold the title to the royal ambassador Diego de Herrera, Prince Henry of Portugal and finally to the Spanish Count Hernán Peraza the Elder, one after the other. This left the possession of the Canaries completely unclear. Both the Spanish and the Portuguese sent ships in the following decades to conquer the islands. Only the **Treaty of Alcáçovas** in 1479 clarified the situation: the Canary Islands were awarded to Spain; Portugal got West Africa and any other offshore islands.

When the Spanish landed on Gran Canaria in 1478 under the leadership of Juan Rejón, the island was ruled by two kings or »guanartemen«, as they were called. Tenesor Semidan, the ruler of the western part, governed from Gáldar; Doramas, the eastern ruler, was based in Telde. The Spanish founded Las Palmas in 1478 and conquered the rest of the island from here. Their capture of Tenesor Semidan was a decisive success. He was brought to Spain along with his entire entourage and baptized. Then he fought on the side of the Spanish conquerors, but only after many more bitter battles under the leadership of Pedro de Vera and Alonso Fernández de Lugo were the Canarians conquered in 1483.

Tile picture at the church plaza in Ingenio – the life of the Canarians was probably not always this idyllic

In 1492–93 the Spanish conquered the island of La Palma. The Guanches on Tenerife held out and kept their independence the longest, but between 1494 and 1496 Alonso Fernández de Lugo also took this, the largest of the Canary Islands.

A large part of the indigenous population was enslaved and taken abroad. The surviving Guanches adapted to Spanish culture at an astonishing pace. Many intermarried with Spanish settlers, took on their language, religion, customs and traditions and adapted to the new economic situation. According to anthropological research most of the present Canarian population is descended from the ancient inhabitants.

Señorio status After the Spanish conquest there were two different systems of administration on the island: while Gran Canaria, La Palma and Tenerife answered directly to the Spanish crown, Fuerteventura, La Gomera, El Hierro and Lanzarote had the status of »señoríos« (_**ounties**) and were subject to the feudal rule of the noblemen who had conquered the islands. The population had to pay taxes to the local ruler and the Spanish empire. Only in 1812 did the Spanish parliament abolish the señorios.

On his first voyage of discovery in 1492, Christopher Columbus (Spanish: Cristóbal Colón, 1451–1506) landed first at Gran Canaria and then La Gomera. On his later voyages (1493, 1498 and 1502) he also stopped at these two islands.

Intermezzo: Columbus

The islands gained economic influence with the cultivation of sugar cane and later wine. Its wealth made Gran Canaria the object of pirate attacks in the 16th and 17th centuries. Time and again the English, Dutch and Portuguese tried to take Las Palmas, but never succeeded.

Pirate attacks

19th and 20th Centuries

1820	Las Palmas becomes the capital of Gran Canaria.
1822	Santa Cruz becomes the capital of the Canary archipelago.
1852	The Canaries become a free trade zone.
1912	The islands gain local autonomy.
1927	The archipelago is divided into an eastern and a western province.
1936–39	Spanish Civil War
1982	The Canary Autonomous Region is formed.

In order to promote the economy of the Canaries, Queen Isabella II of Spain declared the islands to be a free trade zone in 1852.

Free trade zone

In 1912 the »cabildos insulares« were established on the islands, which gave each island its own **local government**. In 1927 the Canary Islands were divided into a western and an eastern province. Since then Tenerife, La Gomera, La Palma and El Hierro have been part of the province of Santa Cruz de Tenerife. The two Canary provinces were combined in 1982 into the »Canarian Autonomous Region«. Like the 16 other Spanish autonomous regions, the Canary Islands gained a regional constitution under a **statute of autonomy** as well as elected representative bodies. Since then the island parliament has met alternately in Santa Cruz de Tenerife and Las Palmas de Gran Canaria.

In July 1936 the Spanish military, including **General Francisco Franco** (1892–1975), who was at that time the military commander of the Canary Islands, revolted against the democratically elected republican government. The preparations for the coup that led to the Spanish Civil War (1936–39) were made on Tenerife. Franco assembled the island's garrison on 17 June 1936 near the town of Esperanza in order to gain their support.

Spanish Civil War

Franco was the military commander on the Canary Islands when the Spanish army revolted against the republican government.

GALICIA GREETS FRANCE!

On 15 July 1936 a twin-engine Dragon Rapide landed at Gando Airport near Las Palmas on Gran Canaria. On board, along with the pilot C.W.H. Bebb, were a retired major, Hugh Pollard, his daughter Diana and her friend Dorothy Watson – en route on a secret mission.

Everything had run according to plan up to that point. Their cover as English tourists seemed to be intact. Pollard and the two girls went on to Santa Cruz de Tenerife. There they went to the Clinica Costa, where they were to meet a certain Dr. Gabarda. Pollard said only one sentence: »Galicia saluda a Francia!« (Galicia greets France!). The doctor looked at the three visitors in astonishment. But the major only repeated the sentence. The doctor lost his temper: he wasn't interested in Galicia greeting France, he retorted. Pollard scraped together what little Spanish he knew, told the doctor that he had orders to tell him that Galicia greets France and that he and his companions would be in the Hotel Pino de Oro. That was the end of the conversation.

Secret Meeting Place

Bebb, the pilot, had stayed behind in the hotel in Las Palmas. He also had unusual encounters. One visitor who introduced himself as Captain Lucena badgered him with questions. For whom and why was he on Gran Canaria; who were his passengers and when was he leaving again? Bebb was suspicious. He had a secret mission. Could he trust the officer? Maybe he was on the other side! He did not want to take any risks, so he answered the questions ingenuously. The Spanish officer finally told him to go to a certain place at a certain time. In a villa in the mountains Bebb met a general named Orgaz and his interpreter, a certain Don Bonny. But the meticulous interrogation of Bebb was just as fruitless as his first conversation with Captain Lucena in the hotel. The two Spaniards were certain that they had the wrong man and sent him away with a warning to forget everything that he had heard.

The Unknown Passenger

On the morning of 18 July Bebb was woken by three Spanish officers and brought to the military command. After waiting for hours, he was told at noon that it was time to go. Outside Bebb saw familiar faces – General Orgaz and Don Bonny. With an armed escort they went to Gando

Airport, where Bebb's Dragon Rapide stood waiting in the middle of the runway. The airplane was ready to take off. Then the passengers appeared – three Spanish officers. One of them, a man in his mid-forties, with silver streaks in his black hair, approached Bebb and introduced himself: »I am General Franco«. Bebb looked at him in astonishment. So this was the mysterious passenger whom he was supposed to take to Spanish Morocco. Bebb did not know who the man really was. General Franco entered the Dragon Rapide at 2.10pm. He exchanged his military uniform for a grey suit, shaved off his moustache and put on sunglasses. One of his co-conspirators gave him a diplomatic passport – in case there were complications during a stopover in French Morocco. On 19 July at 7am Bebb landed the plane in Tetuan, the capital of Spanish Morocco. Luis Botin slapped the English pilot on the shoulder and said: »One day you will understand what you have done for us«. Bebb laughed. He still considered it to be an adventure.

Beginning of the Civil War

When Franco took command of the African forces, Moroccan mercenaries and the foreign legion on 19 July in Tetuan, the rebellion against the government of the Popular Front, which took power in 1936, had already begun in Madrid. Italian and German planes took Franco's soldiers to the Spanish mainland, where they soon conquered large areas with the help of Italian regular troops and the German **Condor Legion**. In September 1936 a junta named the rebel Franco as »generalissimo« and »head of state«. After three years of battles, with atrocities committed on both sides, Madrid fell to Franco's troops in March 1939. The Spanish Civil War was over.

Efforts at autonomy
In the 1970s the autonomy of the Canaries from the Spanish motherland was a major topic in local politics. The separatists blamed the mainland Spanish (and foreigners) for their economic problems. Walls and rocks were covered with the demand of »Fuera Godos« (»Goths out«: members of the Spanish nobility were originally called »Godos« because they claimed to be descended from Visigoth nobles; later all non-Canarians were called Godos). The **separatism movement** climaxed in the years 1976 to 1978, when terrorists tried to enforce the slogan »fuera godos« with bombs. These attempts, which were supported by the Algerian government, did not cause any serious damage.

The situation was defused when the Canaries got a degree of autonomy in 1982 as part of the decentralization policies of the Spanish government. However, the topic of more independence – for example extensive autonomy within a Spanish state – comes up regularly in island politics.

Ties to the EU
When Spain, which was transformed into a constitutional monarchy after the death of Franco in 1975, joined the European Union in 1986, there were initially no economic consequences for the Canary Islands: they had refused to join the EU in order to keep their status as a free trade zone and were the subject of a special agreement due to their location. In 1989 the Canarian parliament decided to join the EU anyway, above all to profit from EU subsidies and infrastructure aid, and to make it possible to export Canarian goods to Europe. The Canary Islands have been completely integrated into the EU since 1993.

Recent Developments

1990	Las Palmas gets a university.
2005	The island is made a biosphere reserve.
Since 2006	Unparalleled immigration from Africa

University town
Decades of conflict in the cultural sector between the two Canary provinces Santa Cruz de Tenerife and Las Palmas de Gran Canaria were ended in 1990 when Las Palmas got its own university.

Political balance of power
The local elections and the **election for the Canarian parliament** in June 2003 were won by the nationalists, the Coalición Canaria. They won 22 of the 60 seats in the parliament. Together with the conservative people's party PP, which got 17 seats, it formed the government, as it had in the previous elections in 1999. Since the coalition fell apart in May 2005 the Coalición Canaria has been ruling as a minority government.

UNESCO declared 43% of the territory of Gran Canaria to be a biosphere reserve.

Biosphere reserve

The Canary Islands experienced an unparalleled invasion of illegal immigrants from Africa in 2006. Almost daily one or more boats full of refugees landed on the coast of Gran Canaria or other islands. When they arrive on the Canaries, the refugees are held by the police for a few days, then sent to refugee camps for 40 days. Many are then flown to the Spanish mainland, while others are taken back to their country of origin.

Illegal immigration

Arts and Culture

Did the Guanches leave an artistic legacy? What does a typical Canarian house look like? Where are the most significant buildings on the island? What is »lucha canaria«?

Ancient Canarian Art

Some ceramic items from pre-Hispanic times have survived. They are free-form and were not made on a potter's wheel. Many have concave handles that also served as spouts. Most of them have smooth surfaces, but on some designs are etched into the surface. The forms varied from island to island. Thus ceramic objects from La Palma are characterized by impressed decoration, while those from Gran Canaria are especially artistic. **Pintaderas** are »stamps« with highly ornamented designs. They were usually ceramic, more rarely made of wood, and were presumably used to »sign« objects. No two pintaderas are completely identical. **Idols** were probably used in religious rites. Almost all that have been preserved are in fragmentary form. The idol of Tara, possibly the oldest Canarian find, is the only one that has artistic value. It was discovered on Gran Canaria and is today in the Museo Canario in Las Palmas. The statue with its grotesquely fat limbs appears female, even though it has no breasts (photo p.36). **Cave paintings** were only found in Cueva Pintada in the north (Gáldar). The cave is decorated with coloured geometric patterns. All in all, there are few artistic items, and these are very plain.

Architecture

Here and there in the interior, one-storey **farmhouses** can be seen. They have 30–40 sq m/300–450 sq ft of living space, but families spent much of their time in the partly covered and luxuriantly planted courtyards. The houses generally face south, so they need no shutters to keep out wind and rain. The single-storey **urban dwellings** are usually small and cramped; two-storey houses have outside steps made of wood or stone, a small balcony or – more rarely – a vestibule. With few exceptions even upper-class houses are relatively small; they hardly differ from more modest two-storey buildings. The shady inner courtyard with many plants forms the focal point of the house, with steps (generally on the left) going up to the living quarters on the top floor. Almost all houses are white-washed. This reflects sunlight, keeps the houses cool and repels insects, which avoid the white surfaces because they cannot hide on them.

The most characteristic features of Canarian architecture are the elaborately carved balconies, windows and doors, all of which are painted green, white or rust-brown; they have always been status symbols. **Balconies** can be divided into two groups: those with shaped wooden balustrades, above which they are open to the roof; and those with a screen going up to the roof in the Arab style, which allows the occupants to look out without being seen. There are also various combinations of these forms.

Urban and rural residences

← *Elaborate entrance to Casa de Colón in Las Palmas*

Architectural History

After the Spanish conquest, European-style and above all Spanish-style churches and other buildings with modest pretensions were constructed. These might not be outstanding examples of architecture, but some of the buildings, which represent a wide variety of styles, are of interest. At first the **Gothic** style was used, for example the ribbed vaulting in the Catedral de Santa Ana in Las Palmas de Gran Canaria. Then Gothic and **Renaissance** elements were combined, as at Casa de Colón in Las Palmas. Gothic or Renaissance style combined with Moorish elements to form the **Mudejar style**. It was developed in Spain by Mudejar architects. i.e. Moors who were »allowed to remain« in the country, but also by Christian builders who were influenced by the Moorish style. Its most important characteristics are horseshoe-shaped arches, stalactite vaulting and stucco or-

Teror is considered to be the most beautiful town on the island.
The houses are decorated with magnificent wooden balconies.

naments. Mudejar style developed into the **Plateresque style**, beginning in the late 15th century in Spain. Façades were given intricate, detailed decorations. The Canary Islands developed a special variety of this style, often incorporating wooden ceilings made of Canary pine. They are richly decorated, in some cases in different colours. In the 17th century **Baroque** architecture appeared, but was used less than the Gothic or Renaissance style on Gran Canaria. However, many of the churches were given a Baroque remodelling. **Classicism** left its mark from the 18th century, mainly in the façades. Austere composition and, compared to Baroque works, restrained use of statuary is expressed in the façade of the Catedral de Santa Ana in Las Palmas. The architecture of the 19th century is a mixture of various historical styles.

A building boom has been in progress on Gran Canaria since the 1960s. Countless giant hotel complexes sprang up, especially in the south of the island. Tourist sites like Maspalomas/Playa del Inglés are planned communities. These aesthetically questionable solutions are points of controversy on the islands as well. Puerto de Mogán, where the two-storey white houses have decorated door and window frames as well as wrought-iron balconies, is generally considered to be an accomplished example of a holiday resort.

Folklore

Fiestas play a central role in life on the Canaries. They generally have religious origins and honour one of the islands' patron saints. As a rule they start with a procession followed by more secular entertainment.

Fiestas

Music plays a large part in these festivities. The songs have passionate rhythms and melodies. Most of the time they are accompanied by a **timple**, a small stringed instrument.

There are grounds in every larger town where **»lucha canaria«** (Canarian wrestling) matches are held. Two wrestlers face off in a circular arena, 9–10m/30–33ft in diameter; each wrestler is part of a twelve-man team. A match consists of three rounds of three minutes each. The winner is the one who wrestles his opponent to the ground twice. **»Juego del palo«**, the Canarian stick fight, requires skill. The two players confront each other with two sticks each and try to hit their opponent according to set rules. The body should be moved as little as possible (▶Baedeker Special, p.94).

Traditional sports

Famous People

Why did Christopher Columbus land on Gran Canaria on his voyages of discovery? Who was the Canary Islands' most famous writer? Who first tried to conquer Gran Canaria?

Jean de Béthencourt (1359–1425)

Jean de Béthencourt from Normandy was given the task of conquering the Canary Islands by Henry III of Castile. Béthencourt was accompanied by **Gadifer de la Salle**, with whom he had gone on a »crusade« against Tunis in 1390.

French conqueror

They gathered a fleet of ships for the expedition and sailed from La Rochelle in 1402. When Béthencourt finally sighted the first islands of the archipelago, he was so happy that he named them Alegranza (joy) and La Graciosa (the graceful one), even though they were barren, rocky places. The adventurers dropped anchor at Lanzarote and took the island in a relatively short time. Béthencourt returned to Spain the same year to get reinforcements. At this time Henry III gave him the title »King of the Canary Islands« – wrongly, in the opinion of Gadifer de la Salle, who took part in no more conquests. Jean de Béthencourt subdued Fuerteventura alone in 1405 and founded the capital Betancuria, which was named after him. A short

time later he also took El Hierro. The French nobleman settled Norman and Spanish farmers on the island; the local population was converted to Christianity. Then Béthencourt tried to conquer Gran Canaria and La Palma, but was driven off by the local people. In 1406 Béthencourt named his nephew **Maciot de Béthencourt** viceroy of the islands. Béthencourt himself returned to France and died there in his castle in Granville in 1425.

Christopher Columbus (1451–1506)

Christopher Columbus (in Italian Cristoforo Colombo, in Spanish Cristóbal Colón), who was born in Genoa, visited the Canary Islands several times while on his voyages of discovery. Columbus went to Lisbon in 1476 in order to pursue his dream of discovering a westward passage to India. When no one was willing to finance him he went on to Spain in 1485. In 1492 Ferdinand of Aragón and his wife Isabella of Castile signed an agreement that would make him viceroy of the discovered lands and give him 10% of the profits from the trip.

Explorer

To this day it is not certain that Columbus actually stopped at Gran Canaria on his first trip (1492–93). If he did so, he stayed not voluntarily but to repair the rudder of the *Pinta*. During this short forced stop he is supposed to have stayed in a house on the site of today's

Casa de Colón in Las Palmas. Columbus left for La Gomera in late August 1492. His logbook shows that he witnessed an eruption of the volcano Teide on Tenerife when sailing by. On La Gomera he took on water and food and met **Beatriz de Bobadilla**. While the residents like to tell about the love affair between the two, there is no historical evidence for it. On his second (1493–96), third (1498–1500) and fourth (1502–04) crossings the discoverer of America stopped at La Gomera and once on El Hierro to take on supplies, but he never revisited Gran Canaria. Columbus returned to Spain from his last trip a sick man and died in 1506 in Valladolid.

Néstor Martín Fernández de la Torre (1887–1938)

Painter

The Néstor Museum in Las Palmas is devoted to the painter Néstor Martín Fernández de la Torre, who was born on 7 February 1887 on Gran Ganaria.

After studying at the school of art in Madrid, Néstor de la Torre travelled throughout Europe. In London he studied the work of the Pre-Raphaelites. His first successes as an artist came in 1908. In the next years Néstor de la Torre made numerous paintings inspired by Symbolism that were displayed in international galleries. He also painted murals like the one in the Teatro Pérez Galdós in Las Palmas or in the casino in Santa Cruz de Tenerife. They often depict idealized versions of the Canarian people. In 1934 Néstor de la Torre started a campaign to revive Canarian folklore and architecture. It was his idea to build Pueblo Canario, a Canarian village, but the idea only materialized in 1939 in Las Palmas – a year after the artist died. Water-colour pictures by Néstor de la Torre served as designs for the buildings. In 1956 the Néstor Museum was opened in Pueblo Canario thanks to a donation by the artist's brothers.

Justus Frantz (b. 1944)

Pianist and conductor

The internationally known pianist and composer is among the most famous interpreters of Viennese music of the classical and Romantic periods. The musician's career began in 1967 when he won a musical competition sponsored by German national television. His international fame as a pianist began in 1970: Frantz played under the direction of **Herbert Karajan** with the Berlin Philharmonic Orchestra. In 1975 he made his debut in the USA with the New York Philharmonic, conducted by Leonard Bernstein. From the late 1980s he began visiting Gran Canaria, finally moving to Monte León, a hill behind Maspalomas where many celebrities have villas. The »**Casa de los Músicos**« soon became a refuge for celebrities. People like Steffi

Graf and former German Chancellor Helmut Schmidt have enjoyed the peace and quiet of the finca that Justus Frantz gradually converted into an organic farm with all sorts of domestic animals and a large orchard. It has a vineyard and produces wine. In 1995 Frantz established the Philharmonia of the Nations, a unique orchestra with 196 musicians from 39 different countries and five continents. The orchestra performs all over the world under his baton, sometimes in unusual places like the pope's summer residence, the ancient theatre of Ephesus or under the dome of the Reichstag in Berlin. Of course, the orchestra also plays on Gran Canaria, the conductor's chosen place of residence.

Alfredo Kraus (1927–1999)

The Spanish tenor Alfredo Kraus, son of an Austrian who emigrated to Gran Canaria after World War I, has the honour of having been born in the most famous house in Las Palmas, the **Casa de Colón**. He first studied engineering but soon turned to singing and completed his studies in Milan. In 1956 he debuted in Cairo as the Duke

Opera singer

of Mantua; he broke through internationally in 1958 when he appeared on stage along with Maria Callas in his native country of Spain. He appeared in all of the world's greatest opera houses, including La Scala in Milan, the New York Metropolitan Opera and the Opéra Bastille in Paris. Kraus was considered to be one of the leading lyrical tenors, and was a specialist in Mozart.

He was active until shortly before his death; in 1998 he gave his farewell performance in Berlin in the title role of Jules Massenet's *Werther*. While he was still alive his hometown of Las Palmas inaugurated the **Auditorio Alfredo Kraus**, today one of the foremost cultural forums on the Canary Islands.

Juan Rejón (d. 1481)

The conqueror of Gran Canaria came from Aragon and served in the Castilian navy under the Catholic Monarchs Ferdinand and Isabella, who appointed him to participate in the conquest of the Can-

Founder of Las Palmas de Gran Canaria

ary Islands. His expedition of three ships set out from Puerto de Santa María near Cadiz in May 1478. On 24 June 1478 Rejón and his men disembarked at Las Isletas. The first camp under palms was the origin of the settlement Real de las Palmas, today's city of Las Palmas de Gran Canaria. Conflicts in the invading party led to the deposition of Rejón as governor of the island. His successor, Pedro de Vera, sent him back to Castile as a prisoner, but Rejón gained his freedom, returned to the Canaries and executed de Vera. Rejón's own life ended in 1481 in an attempt to conquer La Gomera. He was murdered at the behest of a rival conquistador, Hernán Peraza. The conquest of Gran Canaria was completed two years later.

Fernando León y Castillo (1842–1918)

Politician

Fernando León y Castillo from Telde was responsible to a large extent for Gran Canaria's economic upswing. He had gained fame as a politician on Gran Canaria in the 1870s, but his time came in 1881, when he was appointed Spanish foreign minister in Madrid. Here he was able to work to Gran Canaria's advantage over and against the other Canarian islands by supporting the development of the harbour of Las Palmas. In a short time it became the major port of the islands. Fernando's brother, **Juan León y Castillo**, was responsible for planning and supervising the construction of the port. A little museum has been dedicated to both of them in Telde.

José Luján Pérez (1756–1815)

Sculptor and architect

Statues of patron saints by José Luján Pérez can be found in the major churches of Gran Canaria, and also on the entire Canary archipelago. He was born in the little town of Santa María de Guía in northern Gran Canaria. A bust and many wooden Baroque sculptures in the church honour the town's famous son. Luján Pérez worked on his home island not only as a sculptor, but also on the cathedral of Santa Ana as an architect. He designed the classical façade, among other things.

Benito Pérez Galdós (1843–1920)

Author

Benito Pérez Galdós is probably the most famous writer to come from the Canary Islands. The house where he was born on 10 May 1843 in Las Palmas and where he lived as a boy is now a museum. Little is known about his childhood and youth on Gran Canaria. Pérez Galdós was the youngest of many children born to a moderately well-off army officer. After attending school in Las Palmas, he was sent to Madrid in 1863 to study law. He lived there until his death, except when he was making his numerous journeys around Europe. Pérez Galdós only returned to the Canary Islands once. They do not play a role in his works, the most important of which is *Episodios*

Nacionales, the history of Spain in the 19th century told in the form of a 46-volume novel. It was Madrid that really fascinated Pérez Galdós. He wrote in his *Memoirs of an Amnesiac*: »I will skip my childhood since it is uninteresting or at least hardly any different from the experiences of my more or less industrious university years ...«. Pérez Galdós, who as an exponent of Spanish liberalism was controversial during his lifetime, is now considered to be the most important novelist in recent times in Spain. He is best-known internationally through Luis Buñuel's film adaptations of novels such as *Nazarin* (1961).

Practicalities
from A to Z

WOULD YOU LIKE TO KNOW
WHERE THE CANARIOS LOVE
TO EAT, HIKE OR SWIM? WE
HAVE PUT TOGETHER THE BEST
ADDRESSES AND TIPS FOR YOU.

Accommodation

Book from home

The hotel selection on Gran Canaria is practically limitless. There is accommodation for about 160,000 visitors, much of it in **apartments** and bungalows.

Most visitors to the Canaries book package holidays from home. Those who look for accommodation when there will generally pay more but not necessarily get a better room, since the large tour companies often reserve the best rooms for their customers. If you are not travelling during the high season from Christmas to Easter, you should not have any trouble finding a room on your own. Many hotels then only have 25% of their rooms occupied.

Hotels and apartment complexes are divided into **five categories**. The hotels are awarded stars, and the apartments are awarded keys. The standard is based on the quality of the interior and furnishings, not on the quality of the service and food.

Turismo Rural

In order to move away from the image of mass tourism, the Turismo Rural project (Turismo Rural, ▸Baedeker Tip p.127) for holidays in the country has been initiated.

Camping

Camping is not common on Gran Canaria; there are only three campgrounds.

▶ SOME ADDRESSES

TURISMO RURAL

▸ **On Gran Canaria**
Grantural
Calle Perojo 36
Las Palmas
Tel. 928 39 01 69
fax 928 39 01 70
www.ecoturismocanarias.com

CAMPGROUNDS

▸ **Camping Guantánamo**
La Playa de Tauro
near Puerto Rico
Tel. 928 50 62 07

▸ **Camping Temisas**
Lomo de la Cruz
on the road from Agüimes to
San Bartolomé
Tel. 928 79 81 49

▸ **Camping Pasito Blanco**
Pasito Blanco
3 km west of Maspalomas
Tel. 928 14 21 96
Best-equipped campground on the island with restaurant, swimming pool and playground, but *only for camper vans*

Arrival · Before the Journey

Means of Arrival

There are direct **charter flights** to Gran Canaria from all major European airports (flying time approx. 4 hours). **Regular scheduled flights** are worth considering as an alternative, e.g. Air Europa (www.aireuropa.com) from London. There are also connecting flights several times a day from Madrid or Barcelona with Iberia (www.iberia.com).

Once a week (departure Tuesday evening) **ferries** run by the Spanish shipping line **Trasmediterránea** travel the route Cádiz – Santa Cruz de Tenerife – Las Palmas de Gran Canaria. The trip from Cádiz to Gran Canaria takes about two days. Passage can be booked with travel agents.

By air

> **!** *Baedeker* TIP
>
> ### Island hopping
>
> For first-time visitors to the Canaries, a tour including two or three islands is an attractive option. Many travel agencies offer holidays covering several Canary Islands. There is a large selection of air and ferry connections between the islands for those who want to organize the trip themselves (see p.110).

Immigration and Customs Regulations

As the Canary Islands are part of Spain, citizens of EU countries which are party to the Schengen agreement can enter without border checks. However, travellers from the UK and Ireland need a valid identification card or passport. Children under 16 years of age must carry a children's passport or be entered in the parent's passport. For a stay of up to 90 days, citizens of Australia, Canada, New Zealand and the USA do not require a visa.

Travel documents

Always carry your driving licence, the motor vehicle registration and the international green insurance card. Motor vehicles must have the oval sticker showing nationality unless they have a Euro licence plate.

Car documents

Those who wish to bring pets (dogs, cats) require a pet pass. Among other things, it contains an official veterinary statement of health (no more than 30 days old), a rabies vaccination certificate that is at least 30 days and no more than eleven months old, and a passport photo. In addition, the animal must have a microchip or tattoo.

Pets

The Canary Islands have a **special status** within the European Union member states: they are not treated as part of the common economic area within which the movement of goods for private purposes is largely duty-free. This means: the maximum quantities (for example 800 cigarettes, 10 litres of spirits and 90 litres of wine per person)

Customs regulations

◄ Special customs status

ARRIVAL INFORMATION

AIRPORT

▶ **Aeropuerto de Gando**
22km/14mi south of Las Palmas
Tel. 9 28 57 91 30
Taxi: ca. 25 Euros to Las Palmas or
Maspalomas
Bus: Global bus no. 60 runs
between 6am and 7pm every 30
minutes, between 8pm and
1.30am every hour to Parque San
Telmo in Las Palmas.

FERRIES

▶ **Trasmediterránea**
Estación Marítima
Muelle de Ribera
Santa Cruz de Tenerife
Tel. 922 84 22 44
www.trasmediterranea.com

applicable for journeys between other parts of the EU do not apply. Instead it is possible to take in and out the quantities of duty-free goods that apply for travel between EU states and non-EU states: for persons over the age of 15 500g of coffee and 100g of tea, 50g of perfume and 0.25 litres of eau de toilette, and for persons over the age of 17 1 litre of spirits over 22% or 2 litres of spirits under 22% or 2 litres of sparkling wine and 2 litres of wine, as well as 200 cigarettes or 50 cigars or 250g of tobacco. Goods with a maximum value of 430 euros may be imported.

Health Insurance

Citizens of EU countries are entitled to treatment on Gran Canaria under the local regulations in case of illness on production of their **European health insurance card**. Those who do not have one should bring an alternative health certificate. Even with this card, in most cases some of the costs for medical care and prescribed medication must be paid by the patient. Upon presentation of receipts the health insurance at home covers the costs – but not for all treatments.

Private
travel insurance

Since some of the costs for medical treatment and medication typically have to be met by the patient, and the costs for return transportation may not be covered by the normal health insurance, additional travel insurance is recommended.

Beaches

Beach paradise

Gran Canaria's most beautiful beaches are in the south near Maspalomas or Playa del Inglés. The quality of the water here is excellent.

In the tourist centres topless sunbathing is common, but this is bound to attract attention on beaches frequented only by the local people. Nude bathing is tolerated on more remote beaches. Nudists should go to the dunes near Maspalomas or Playa del Inglés.

Guests at the hotels around the former fishing village of Arguineguín have to make do with a tiny beach; the well-kept swimming pools look more attractive.

Arguineguin

North-west of Las Palmas lies the 2km/1¼mi-long **Playa de las Canteras**, one of the largest urban public beaches in the world. Rock reefs form a barrier against the surf and swimming here is safe. Even though the beach and the promenade are well cared for, it is impossible to forget that the beach is in a city: at weekends it is overcrowded, and the industrial zone begins at the southern end of Playa de las Canteras.

Las Palmas

An 8km/5mi-long, well-tended beach of white sand stretches from the lighthouse at El Oasis to Playa del Inglés. It is bordered by impressive dunes that are under nature protection. This fascinating coastal scenery is **Gran Canaria's main attraction**. In the winter months masses of sun-starved Europeans come here. A never-ending line of beachcombers walks along the edge of the water then – all day, every day. In many places loungers, sunshades, paddleboats, surfboards etc. can be rented; there are countless simple snack bars along the beach.

Playa del Inglés/ Maspalomas

> ### *i* The most beautiful beaches
>
> - Playa del Inglés: the most famous beach on the Canary Islands
> - Playa de las Canteras: the public beach of Las Palmas, often compared to the Copacabana in Rio
> - Playa de los Amadores: an artificial but wonderful beach
> - Playa de Güigüí: a secluded but fabulous beach, only accessible on foot or by boat

Puerto de las Nieves is the only place in north-western Gran Canaria with an adequate beach. The stretch of dark sand is about 100m/100yd long and 25m/25yd wide, and mainly used by local people.

Puerto de las Nieves

Puerto de Mogán has a small beach of light-coloured sand. Breakwaters make it possible for children to splash around safely. Alternatives are **Playa del Taurito** to the east, which is now surrounded by resort facilities, or **Playa de Veneguera**. This dark and rocky beach has been earmarked as the site of another development. The ultimate beach experience can be found at **Playa de Güigüí** (▶ Baedeker Special, p.192), which is only accessible on foot or by boat.

Puerto de Mogán

The beach at Puerto Rico does have one huge advantage: the sun is usually still shining here when Maspalomas or Playa del Inglés are already covered by clouds. Since this is often the case in the winter,

Puerto Rico

Beach at Puerto Rico: the best places are taken early

this beach can get crowded then. Even at other times the 400m/ 450yd-long artificial beach seems to be paved with beach loungers. Swimmers share the water with numerous surfers, sailors and yachts. Rock reefs prevent the surf from getting too powerful.

Playa de los Amadores west of Puerto Rico provides some relief from the congestion. This artificial beach is one of the most beautiful on the island.

San Agustín Compared to the adjacent Playa del Inglés, the beach of San Agustín is more modest. There are several small coves for swimming. The white sandy beach in front of the Sun Club is the best; other sections have only dark sand.

Children on Gran Canaria

Very child- Many hoteliers and travel agents on Gran Canaria have specialized in
friendly arrangements for children: reduced rates, children's menus, child-minding and much more is available at some hotels and holiday apartments. Many beaches are protected by breakwaters so that the surf is reduced or the water is almost completely calm. The beaches Playa de Mogán, Playa Taurito and Playa de los Amadores are well suited for children since they shelve gently.

Kids almost always love a **boat trip** (► Excursions); in Puerto de Mogán the »Yellow Submarine« makes trips every hour. Animal rides are also offered in several places: near ► Fataga there are two **camel safaris**, as well as one by the dune lake near the lighthouse at Maspalomas. **Horseback riding** is available at Rancho Park (► Playa del Inglés). A »**burro safari**« goes through Barranco de Guayadeque; the price includes a lunch.

i Top tips for children

- Aqua Sur: an outstanding water park where everyone joins in
- Palmitos Park: shark tank, birds of prey and parrot shows
- Safari Maspalomas: sway through the dunes on a dromedary
- Sioux City: Wild West on Gran Canaria
- Yellow Submarine: go under water in a submarine

There are also various theme parks to choose from. The water parks provide an alternative when the sea is too rough for a day on the beach. In addition Palmitos Park and Sioux City are also popular. The admission charges tend to be somewhat high (approx. 8–20 € for adults). Most of the parks are in the south.

Theme parks

There is a minigolf course in San Valentin Park in Playa del Inglés (in Calle Timple, near the intersection of Avenida de Tirajana and Avenida de Gran Canaria. Hours: daily 9am–11pm).

Minigolf

Something for big and little kids: Sioux City near San Agustín

● ATTRACTIONS FOR CHILDREN

ZOOS/
BOTANICAL GARDENS

▶ **Cactualdea**
　▶ San Nicolás de Tolentino
Cactus park

▶ **Palmitos Park**
　▶ Maspalomas
Subtropical park with more than
1000 birds, parrot show

▶ **Parque de Cocodrilos**
　▶ Agüimes
Small zoo with crocodile and
parrot show

▶ **Reptilandia**
　▶ Agaete
Outdoor terrariums with
reptiles

▶ **Jardín Canario**
　▶ Tafira
Large botanical garden with
Canarian flora

OPEN-AIR MUSEUM

▶ **Mundo Aborigen**
　▶ Playa del Inglés
In the footsteps of the Guanches

AMUSEMENT AND
THEME PARKS

▶ **Holiday World**
　▶ Maspalomas
Ferris wheel, carousels, many
other attractions and shows

▶ **Sioux City**
　▶ San Agustín
Artificial Wild West town

WATER PARKS

▶ **Ocean Park**
Campo Internacional
Maspalomas

Motorway exit no. 47
Various water slides, wave pool,
restaurants
Hours: daily 10am–6pm

▶ **Aqua Sur**
Near Maspalomas
on the road to Palmitos Park
On 130,000 sq m/32 acres there
are ten attractions and 29 water
slides, as well as a minigolf course.
Hours: daily 10am–6pm

▶ **Agua Park**
Avenida Tomás Roca, Puerto
Rico Water park with many water
slides
Hours: daily 10am–5.30pm or
6.30pm in the summer

GO-KART

▶ **Go-Kart Racing**
2km/1¼mi north-west of
Maspalomas (towards El Tablero)
Junior karts, special karts, racing
karts and double karts are available; children especially like the
»bumper boats« (motorized
boats); observation terrace with
restaurant.
Hours: daily 10am–11pm

▶ **Gran Karting Club**
Tarajalillo, San Agustín
Go-karts for all ages: there is a
children's track with mini karts for
children from the age of 5; for
children from 10 years there are
»mini-bikes«; for ages 12–16 there
is a junior track and for older
children a 1650m/1800yd-long
track.
Hours: daily 11am–10pm (in
winter until 9pm)

Electricity

Gran Canaria uses 220 volt electricity; an adapter is generally necessary for visitors from the UK and Ireland. These are available at local shops and called »adaptador« or »ladrón« in Spanish.

Emergency

 IMPORTANT TELEPHONE NUMBERS

EMERGENCY NUMBERS
▶ **Fire department, police, doctor**
Tel. 902 102 112

▶ **Multilingual police**
Tel. 112

Entertainment

There are three casinos on Gran Canaria: the Gran Casino Costa Meloneras with 17 gaming tables and 100 slot machines on the Costa Meloneras was opened in 2005. There is another casino in the Hotel Tamarindos (San Agustín) and a third in the Hotel Santa Catalina (Las Palmas). They offer French and American roulette, baccarat, black jack and other games.

Casinos

Internationally known musicians perform in the Auditorio Alfredo Kraus in Las Palmas

Nightclubs In Gran Canaria's tourist centres, especially in **Playa del Inglés**, there are many nightclubs. Flamenco shows are sometimes held in the nightclub Aladinos in Playa del Inglés. The revue in the Casino Palace (in Hotel Tamarindos; San Agustín) is good (reservations recommended, tel. 9 28 76 27 24).

Etiquette

Spanish politeness Spanish people are generally polite, and this courtesy permeates their daily life. They like to chat at length, listen to other opinions patiently and of course try to persuade others. They are accomplished in word and gesture, but not know-alls. If someone in the office said, »The new guy is called Pedro« no one would disagree and say »No, no, his name is José«. The elegant Spanish version would be: »José? or Pedro?« If the polite Spaniard cannot comply with a request, wish or demand, he has a problem. He would never just say »No!«. An example: a visitor in a small town asks his host for the closest car rental agency. The host knows that none is anywhere nearby, but would never say so; instead he says »That is difficult«. This means »Forget it!«

Puerto de las Nieves: Canarian families come here at weekends

Invitations are extended quickly and happily, but guests are rarely in-vited home. Instead they are invited to bars or restaurants, where people do not linger and move on quickly. Spaniards do not like to go out alone, rather in small or large groups. If someone brings a friend to the nightly gathering, he is quickly accepted and integrated into the group. This applies to foreigners as well. But do not expect a deeper friendship if someone casually says »Call me sometime« when leaving. He doesn't expect to hear from you on the very next day.

The bar is the living room

The Spanish rule for paying the bill in bars or restaurants is that one person always pays the entire bill. If a group moves from place to place each member takes a turn at the bill. The bill is not divided to the last penny; **generosity** is expected. As a foreigner in a group of Spaniards you might even have problems taking your turn. Someone else will always have beaten you to it.

One for all

There is another restaurant rule: never sit down at a table with a stranger. The question »Is this place free?« is simply not asked. But do not sit at a vacant table either: wait for the head waiter to come, ask for the number of guests and suggest a table. Then guests are guided to the table and given menus.

»Is this place free?«

The **bill** is requested casually. It will arrive on a small plate and the waiter will leave again. Someone will casually reach for the bill, glance at it and place cash or a credit card on the plate. The waiter will return just as casually and take the plate while murmuring »Gra-cias«. After a while he will return and place the plate with the change in front of the payer with another »Gracias«. He in turn ignores it for a few seconds, then pockets the change and leaves the tip on the plate. The waiter will only pick up the tip when all the guests have left the table.

Rituals for paying bills

Excursions

Along with the trip around the island, the most popular excursions include trips to the mountains, to Agaete, Tejeda or to Palmitos Park as well as shopping trips to Las Palmas or on Sundays to markets in the smaller towns. Organizing your own bus trip needs a bit of time and patience, but all larger towns are accessible by public transporta-tion (►Transport).

By bus

Gran Canaria is best explored with a rental car (►Tours). Organized Jeep safaris are a enjoyable way to explore the island, as they go to untouched areas that are not accessible to normal cars.

By car

By boat   The range of boating excursions covers everything from short trips to day trips to cruises lasting several days. Trips for shark fishing or on the sailing ship *San Miguel* (from Puerto Rico) are popular. The »Yellow Submarine« leaves from Puerto de Mogán on trips to the world under the sea. There is regular boat passage between Puerto Rico and Puerto de Mogán and Arguineguín. A ride on a high-speed boat is also suitable for a day trip between Las Palmas (Gran Canaria) and Santa Cruz (Tenerife). A ferry covers the distance from Santa Cruz to Puerto de las Nieves in an hour. A side trip to Fuerteventura is also possible. Day trips by boat to other islands are not worthwhile because of the distances (▶Transport).

> ### 𝑖 Shopping trips
>
> ■ On Gran Canaria visitors are inundated by offers for »free shopping trips« – there is clearly still plenty of money to be made from tourists!

Since each of the Canary Islands has its own character, trips to another island provide variety and thanks to the low cost of air tickets are an affordable holiday pleasure (▶ Transport). Agents also offer short **flights** to Gambia or Marrakech in Morocco. Anyone who wants to see Gran Canaria from the air should go to **Blue Canarias Helicopters** (see Baedeker Tip p.198).

Festivals, Holidays and Events

Canarians love to celebrate   Every town has its own fiesta in honour of the local patron saint. In the summer months there is always a festival going on somewhere. The fiestas all have more or less the same pattern. The religious part comes first, a church service and then a procession (**vomería**) on streets decorated for the event with local people wearing elaborate costumes. Then the secular events and entertainment follow: folklore groups dance and sing, a fair and sporting events

> ### 𝑖 You can't miss it!
>
> ■ Carnival: the only bigger one is in Rio
> ■ Music festival: top-quality soloists and orchestras in Las Palmas
> ■ Bajada de la Rama: one of the island's typical folk festivals
> ■ Fiesta del Charco: can't be topped

like the »lucha canaria« take place. The climax is the »verbena«, a dance at night that lasts into the morning hours. The festival often concludes with fireworks.

If the saint's feast day falls in the middle of the week the festival is generally moved to the preceding or following weekend so that at least two nights are free for celebrating. Festivals can even last for several days.

FESTIVALS AND EVENTS

PUBLIC HOLIDAYS

▶ **1 January**
Año Nuevo (New Year)

▶ **5 and 6 January**
Los Reyes
(Epiphany)

▶ **19 March**
San José (feast of St Joseph)

▶ **1 May**
Día del Trabajo
(Labour Day)

▶ **30 May**
Día de las Islas Canarias
(Canary Island Day)

▶ **25 July**
Santiago Apóstol
(feast of the St James)

▶ **15 August**
Asunción
(feast of the Assumption of the
Virgin)

▶ **12 October**
Día de la Hispanidad (discovery of
America; national holiday)

▶ **1 November**
Todos los Santos (All Saints' Day)

▶ **6 December**
Día de la Constitución
(Constitution Day)

▶ **8 December**
Inmaculada Concepción
(Immaculate Conception)

▶ **25 December**
Navidad (Christmas)

▶ **Movable holidays**
Viernes Santo (Good Friday)
Día del Corpus (Corpus Christi)

> ! *Baedeker* TIP
>
> **Festivals and dates**
> An up-to-date calendar of events including
> the best island festivals, but also exhibitions,
> sporting events, concerts, theatre and much
> more is available in three languages under
> www.vivecanarias.com.

JANUARY

▶ **Cabalgada de los Reyes**
On the evening of 5 January the
arrival of the Magi is celebrated in
Las Palmas. Children receive
presents in the evening or on the
following day, not at Christmas.

JANUARY/FEBRUARY

▶ **Festival de Música de Canarias**
Internationally known orchestras
and soloists take part in the
festival of classical music. Performances take place in the Auditorio Alfredo Kraus in Las Palmas.

FEBRUARY/MARCH

▶ **Carnival**
Carnival is celebrated extrava-
gantly in many towns. The uncontested centre is Las Palmas (see
Baedeker Tipp p.73).

▶ **Fiestas del Almendro en Flor**
Almond blossom festival in Tejeda
and Valsequillo

▶ **Festival de Opera**
Right after the music festival the
opera festival takes place in the
capital.

It's like Rio at the Gran Cabalgata, the carnival parade in Las Palmas

MARCH/APRIL

▶ **Semana Santa**
Holy Week sees numerous processions and other religious as well as secular events.

▶ **Fiesta de Ansite**
On 29 April in Santa Lucia this festival commemorates the last resistance of the original Canarians against the Spanish conquerors at Fortaleza de Ansite.

MAY

▶ **Fiesta del Albaricoque**
The apricot festival in early May signals the beginning of the apricot harvest with dancing, fireworks and a craft show.

MAY/JUNE

▶ **Corpus Christi**
Corpus Christi is celebrated with processions and elaborate carpets of flowers and volcanic earth; the celebrations are especially impressive in Las Palmas and Arucas. So that everyone can take part, it is celebrated a week later than the actual date of Corpus Christi.

JUNE

▶ **El Día de San Juan**
24 June, the feast of St John, is the founding day of Las Palmas. It is celebrated every year with many events.

JULY

▶ **International jazz festival**
in Auditorio Alfredo Kraus in Las Palmas

▶ **Fiesta de Nuestra Señora del Carmen**
Feast of the patron saints of Las Palmas, Gáldar and San Nicolás de Tolentino, celebrated on 16 July with boat parades

▶ **Fiesta de Santiago Apóstol**
From 15 to 30 July in San Bartolomé de Tirajana the feast of St James is celebrated.

AUGUST

▶ **Bajada de la Rama**

This is one of the leading folklore festivals on the Canaries and is celebrated in Agaete from 4 to 7 August. The »lowering of the branches« goes back to an ancient Canarian custom in which the gods are beseeched to supply enough water for the harvest. Today it is still customary to climb into the hills, bring back a pine branch, and beat the water with it at the beach.

SEPTEMBER

▶ **Fiesta de la Virgen del Pino**

8 September in Teror. Typical pilgrimage, the definitive island event. Many towns have made this a local holiday.

▶ **Fiesta del Charco**

The »pond festival« takes place on 10 September in San Nicolás de Tolentino. Great fun to be had by all (see Baedeker Tip p.199).

OCTOBER

▶ **Fiesta de la Naval**

In the harbour of Las Palmas on 6 October the Spanish victory over the fleet of Sir Francis Drake in 1595 is celebrated.

! Baedeker TIP

Carnival in Las Palmas

No other festival is celebrated as elaborately on Gran Canaria and with as much enthusiasm – just like Rio. The large events, like the election of a carnival queen, take place at the giant open-air stage in Santa Catalina Park. The Drag Queen Gala is the absolute highlight of the carnival. Fates are available at tourist offices or at www.laspalmascarnaval.com.

▶ **Fiesta de Nuestra Señora de la Luz**

Pilgrimage and procession to the sea in Las Palmas on the second Saturday in October

NOVEMBER

▶ **Womad Festival**

For four days world music stars perform in Parque Santa Catalina in Las Palmas.

DECEMBER

▶ **Fiestas de Navidad**

In Las Palmas especially there is a varied selection of pre-Christmas and Christmas events with exhibitions and performances. The exhibition of nativity scenes in Ingenio is worth seeing (see Baedeker Tip p.149).

Food and Drink

The large hotels and most of the restaurants on the island serve **international cuisine**; occasionally »papas arrugadas con mojo«, small wrinkled potatoes with a spicy sauce, might appear. Off the tourist path Canarian cuisine has had a sort of renaissance, but don't expect too much: the cooking is not very sophisticated. As long as you have no false expectations you might be surprised at how good the fresh seafood or hearty fish dishes taste. Canarian cooking has clearly been influenced by the mother country, and typical Spanish ingredients are used: lots of olive oil, garlic and many spices.

No culinary highlights ...

Canarian Dishes

Soups: often a main dish

The fish soup (cazuela de pescado) is especially recommended along the coast; the best kinds also have various shellfish and vegetables along with a variety of fish. An »escaldón« is a porridge-like soup with gofio, and »potaje de verduras« is a thickened vegetable soup. Garlic-lovers should try »sopa de ajos«, garlic soup.

Tapas

Tapas, much loved in mainland Spain, have also been well received on the Canaries. These little **appetizers** are served as starters or a be-tween-meal snack. Tapas bars have a wide selection, from a bite of air-dried ham or salami and a spoon-ful of potato salad to an excellent seafood cocktail or a piece of mari-nated fish.

The focal point of local cuisine is **fish** (pescado), usually grilled or fried. »Vieja« (parrot fish) is a very tasty fish similar to carp. It is pre-pared either fresh or air-dried. »Dorada« (dorado) and »mero« (grouper) are also common. Freshly caught fish of the day is a good but usually not a cheap choice even (or especially) in the simplest restaurants.

Meat dishes

Lovers of meat (carne) should look for pork (cerdo), lamb (cordero), goat (cabrito) as well as rabbit (conejo) on the menus. Like fish, meat is often served grilled or fried, but there are also more unusual local meat dishes, including »puchero«. This stew is made of many different kinds of meat and vegetables. The dishes are spiced with salt, pepper, bay leaves and herbs. Another popular stew is »rancho canario«, which is made with chickpeas, potatoes, noodles, beef and chicken, often also with bacon.

Potatoes are best

The side dish of choice is »**papas arrugadas**«, potatoes cooked in their skins in very salty water. The salt forms a white crust on the skin, which is also eaten.

Mojo is a must

The potatoes are served with a red and a green sauce. These spicy sauces are made with local herbs, garlic, vinegar and oil. If saffron and red chillies are used it is called »mojo rojo«, while the green ver-sion »mojo verde« contains parsley and coriander.

Gofio: staple of the native Canarians

The staple of the ancient inhabitants is still a regular part of the diet today, even if it is rarely seen on a menu. Gofio is made of roasted wheat, corn or barley flour and served with meals in place of bread. It can be either sweet or salty.

The highlights of Canarian cooking are papas arrugadas – small potatoes – and mojo sauces

Since the Canarians love sweet foods, dessert is a regular part of the main meal. Tempting and fattening examples are »bienmesabe« (whipped almond pudding with eggs and honey), »turrones« (almond cake), »flan« (cream caramel), »frangollo« (made of milk and corn) and of course »helados« (ice cream) as well as fresh fruit.

The local springs produce excellent **mineral water** (agua mineral). It is available still (con gas) or sparkling (sin gas).
Beer (cerveza) is often drunk with meals. Many imported beers are available and many restaurants have German or Danish beer on tap, but the Canarian beers are also good. The Tropical brewery is located on Gran Canaria, Dorada on Tenerife.

Wine is the second most popular beverage among the Canarians. On Gran Canaria only a few hundred acres of vineyards remain, near Tafira. The wine is of average quality. The supermarkets sell wines from Lanzarote and Tenerife, mostly simple table wines.

? DID YOU KNOW ...?

■ For the Canarios breakfast consists of café con leche, coffee with milk, and the midday meal is all the more generous. It usually starts between 1pm and 2pm and can last well into the afternoon, especially at weekends. The evening meal thus takes place late. Canarios are rarely seen in a restaurant before 8pm. Hotels and restaurants accommodate European visitors and begin serving at 6pm already.

Every restaurant has its own paella recipe

A meal is usually finished off with **coffee**. It is served as »café solo« (black), »café cortado« (with a little milk) or »café con leche« (coffee with more milk). Another variation is »carajillo« (black coffee with a shot of brandy or rum).

Eating in a Restaurant

Restaurante, bar or bar-restaurante?

There is large selection of restaurants in the tourist centres on Gran Canaria; recommended restaurants are listed under »Sights from A to Z« at the respective location.

Restaurants in Spain are classified not with stars but with forks (1–3), but the forks do not reflect the quality of the food – the criteria for **classification** are the range of choice, the interior furnishings etc. The food in a simple restaurant with only one »fork« can be as good as or even better than the food in a restaurant with three »forks«. Moreover few restaurants make use of the official forks.

Along with **restaurants**, which can be expensive (especially in the tourist centres), there are other ways to satisfy your hunger. In a **bar** – nothing more than the local pub – there is always something to snack on, as a large selection of tapas is usually available. These snacks are eaten while standing at the bar or seated at a little table, if available. A »**bar-restaurante**« has more tables and a larger selection – drinks and tapas are served at the bar and meals at the tables. Often »raciones«, a double portion of tapas, are served.

> ### ⓘ Price categories
>
> ■ The restaurants mentioned in »Sights from A to Z« are divided into the following price categories (price of a main course):
>
> **Expensive**: from 20 €
> **Moderate**: 12 – 20 €
> **Inexpensive**: up to 12 €

Ordering is not much of a problem, as menus are almost always multilingual. It is not usual to share the bill: either tell the staff before ordering that separate bills are required or divide it up yourself after paying it (► etiquette). The bill covers all extra charges, but good service should be rewarded with a 5–10% tip.

Menu, bill

Health

Gran Canaria has adequate medical facilities. Most doctors speak at least one foreign language. In an emergency contact one of the health centres listed below, where many English-speaking doctors work, or the university clinic.

Medical help

Citizens of the EU are entitled to receive treatment in Spain according to the local regulations (►Arrival · Before the Journey).

Medical insurance

Pharmacies (»farmacias«) can be found in all larger towns on Gran Canaria. They are recognizable by the red or green Maltese cross. Opening hours are Mon–Fri 9am–1pm and 4pm–8pm and Sat 9am–1pm. At other times there is a pharmacy with emergency hours. The address is posted in each pharmacy and called »Farmacia de Guardia«. After 10pm medicines are only dispensed on prescription.

Pharmacies

► USEFUL ADDRESSES

EMERGENCY
Tel. 112

HOSPITALS AND MEDICAL CENTRES

► **Hospital Universítaria de Gran Canaria Dr. Negrín**
Calle Barranco de la Ballena
Las Palmas
Tel. 928450000

► **Clínica Roca**
Calle Buganvillas 1
San Agustín
Tel. 928769004
www.clinicaroca.com
24-hour service

► **Clínica Salus**
Avenida de Tenerife 24
Centro Comercial Kasbah
Playa del Inglés
Tel. 928762992
www.gruposalus.com
Other clinics can be found in Maspalomas, Playa Taurito, Playa del Cura and Puerto Rico

ENGLISH-SPEAKING DOCTORS

► **British Medical Clinic**
Avenide Roca Bosch s/n
Bungalows Martinica 19
Costa Rica
Tel. 928 56 00 16
www.britishmedicalclinic.com

Information

● USEFUL ADDRESSES

SPANISH TOURIST OFFICES

▶ **In Canada**
Spanish Tourist Office
Bloor Street West 2-Suite 3402
Toronto, Ontario M4W 3E2
Tel. +1 4169613131
Fax +1 4169611992
www.tourspain.toronto.on.ca

▶ **In Ireland**
Spanish Tourist Office
PO Box 10015, Dublin 1
Tel. 0818 22 02 90
dublin@tourspain.es

▶ **In the UK**
Spanish Tourist Office
PO Box 4009
London W1A 6NB
Tel. 020 7486 8077
www.spain.info

▶ **In the United States**
Spanish Tourist Office
Fifth Avenue 666 - 35th floor
N.Y. 10103 New York
Tel. +1 2122658822
Fax +1 2122658864
www.okspain.org

▶ **Spanish Tourist Office**
Wilshire Blvd. 8383 - Suite 960
Beverly Hills California 90211
Tel. (1323) 658 71 95
Fax 658 10 61
losangeles@tourspain.es

▶ **On Gran Canaria**
Patronato Insular de Turismo
Calle León y Castillo 17, Las Palmas
Tel. 9 28 36 22 22, fax 9 28 36 28 22

Centro Insular de Turismo
Avenida España, Yumbo Center
Playa del Inglés
Tel. 9 28 76 25 91
Hours: Mon–Fri 9am–9pm, Sat
until 1pm

The addresses of the tourist offices
in the tourist centres are listed
under each location under »Sights
from A to Z«.

CONSULATES

▶ **Republic of Ireland**
León y Castillo 195
Las Palmas de Gran Canaria
Tel. 9 28 29 77 28

▶ **United Kingdom**
Calle Luis Morote 6
Las Palmas de Gran Canaria
Tel. 9 28 26 25 08
lapal-consular@fco.gov.uk

▶ **USA**
Calle Martinez de Escobar 3
Las Palmas de Gran Canaria
Tel. 9 28 27 12 59
canarias@bitmailer.net

INTERNET

▶ **www.spain.info**
Internet address of the Spanish
Tourist Office; information on the
Canary Islands.

▶ **www.grancanaria.com**
Official website of the Gran
Canaria tourist association, much
useful information.

▶ **www.vivecanarias.com**
Good for practical information on entertainment and events

▶ **www.abcanarias.com**
General information on all of the Canary Islands. Search engine for hotels and holiday apartments, useful listings for leisure, sport and transport.

▶ **www.ecoturismocanarias.com**
Information on the natural environment and rural accommodation

Language

The staff of larger hotels and restaurants generally speak English. Only in smaller towns in the interior might there be problems in communicating.

The vowels a, e, i, o, u, are short and open in Spanish. There are no long vowels.

Spanish pronunciation

SPANISH PHRASES

At a glance

Yes./No.	Sí./No.
Maybe.	Quizás./Tal vez.
OK!	¡De acuerdo!/¡Está bien!
Please./Thank you.	Por favor./Gracias.
Thank you very much!	Muchas gracias.
You're welcome.	No hay de qué./De nada.
Excuse me!	¡Perdón!
Pardon?	¿Cómo dice/dices?
I don't understand you.	No le/la/te entiendo.
I only speak a little ...	Hablo sólo un poco de ...
Could you help me?	¿Puede usted ayudarme, por favor?
I would like ...	Quiero .../Quisiera ...
I (don't) like that.	(No) me gusta.
Do you have ...?	¿Tiene usted ...?
How much does this cost?	¿Cuánto cuesta?
What time is it?	¿Qué hora es?

Getting acquainted

Good morning	¡Buenos días!
Good day!	¡Buenos días!/¡Buenas tardes!
Good evening!	¡Buenas tardes!/¡Buenas noches!

Hello!	¡Hola! ¿Qué tal?
My name is …	Me llamo …
What is your name, please?	¿Cómo se llama usted, por favor?
How are you?	¿Qué tal está usted?/¿Qué tal?
Fine, thanks. And you?	Bien, gracias. ¿Y usted/tú?
Good bye!	¡Hasta la vista!/¡Adiós!
See you!	¡Adiós!/¡Hasta luego!
See you soon!	¡Hasta pronto!
See you tomorrow!	¡Hasta mañana!

Travelling

left/right	a la izquierda/a la derecha
straight ahead	todo seguido/derecho
close/far	cerca/lejos
How far is it?	¿A qué distancia está?
I would like to rent … .	Quisiera alquilar …
… a car	…un coche.
… a boat	…una barca/un bote/un barco.
Excuse me, where is …?	Perdón, ¿dónde está …
… the railway station	…la estación (de trenes)?
… the bus terminal	…la estación de autobuses/ la terminal?
… the airport	…el aeropuerto?

Breakdown

I had a breakdown.	Tengo una avería.
Would you please send me a towtruck?	¿Pueden ustedes enviarme un cochegrúa, por favor?
Is there a garage here?	¿Hay algún taller por aquí cerca?
Where is the next petrol station?	¿Dónde está la estación de servicio/a gasolinera más cercana, por favor?
I would like … litres of …	Quisiera … litros de …
… normal petrol.	… gasolina normal.
… super./ …diesel.	… súper./ … diesel.
… unleaded./ …leaded.	… sin plomo./ … con plomo.
Fill it up, please.	Lleno, por favor.

Accident

Help!	¡Ayuda!, ¡Socorro!
Careful!	¡Atención!
Careful!	¡Cuidado!
Please call … quickly	Llame enseguida …

Sometimes a few words of Spanish help to get a conversation going

... an ambulance.	... una ambulancia.
... the police.	... a la policía.
... the fire department.	... a los bomberos.
Do you have any bandages?	¿Tiene usted botiquín de urgencia?
It was my (your) fault.	Ha sido por mi (su) culpa.
Please tell me your name and your address.	¿Puede usted darme su nombre y dirección?

Going out

Where is there ...	¿Dónde hay por aquí cerca ...
... a good restaurant?	... un buen restaurante?
... a reasonable restaurant?	... un restaurante no demasiado caro?
Please make a reservation for us for this evening	¿Puede reservarnos para esta noche
for a table for 4 people.	una mesa para cuatro personas?

Cheers!	¡Salud!
The bill, please!	¡La cuenta, por favor!
Did it taste good?	¿Le/Les ha gustado la comida?
The food was excellent.	La comida estaba écelente.

Shopping

Where can I find ... a market?	Por favor, ¿dónde hay ... un mercado?
... a pharmacy	.... una farmacia
... a shopping centre	... un centro comercial

Accommodation

Could you please recommend ... ?	Perdón, señor/señora/señorita. ¿Podría usted recomendarme ...
... a hotel	... un hotel?
... a guesthouse	... una pensión?
I have reserved a room.	He reservado una habitación.
Do you still have ...	¿Tienen ustedes ...?
... a single room?	... una habitación individual?
... a double room?	... una habitación doble?
... with shower/bath?	... con ducha/baño?
... for one night?	... para una noche?
... for one week?	... para una semana?
How much does the room cost	¿Cuánto cuesta la habitación
... with breakfast?	... con desayuno?
... with half board?	... media pensión?

Doctor and pharmacy

Can you recommend a good doctor?	¿Puede usted indicarme un buen médico?
I have ...	Tengo ...
... diarrhea.	... diarrea.
... a fever.	... fiebre.
... a headache.	... dolor de cabeza.
... a toothache.	... dolor de muelas.
... a sore throat.	... dolor de garganta.

Bank

Where is ...	Por favor, ¿dónde hay por aquí...?
... a bank?	... un banco?
... a currency exchange?	... una oficina/casa de cambio?

I would like to change	Quisiera cambiar …
British pounds into euros.	libras británicas

Post

How much does … cost?	¿Cuánto cuesta …
… a letter …	… una carta …
… a postcard …	… una postal …
to Great Britain/USA?	para Inglaterra/ los Estados Unidos?
a stamp	sellos
a telephone card	tarjetas para el teléfono

Numbers

0	cero	19	diecinueve
1	un, uno, una	20	veinte
2	dos	21	veintiuno(a)
3	tres	22	veintidós
4	cuatro	30	treinta
5	cinco	40	cuarenta
6	seis	50	cincuenta
7	siete	60	sesenta
8	ocho	70	setenta
9	nueve	80	ochenta
10	diez	90	noventa
11	once	100	cien, ciento
12	doce	200	doscientos, -as
13	trece	1000	mil
14	catorce	2000	dos mil
15	quince	10 000	diez mil
16	dieciséis		
17	diecisiete	1/2	medio
18	dieciocho	1/4	un cuatro

Restaurant/Restaurante

desayuno	breakfast
almuerzo	lunch
cena	dinner
camarero	waiter
cubierto	setting
cuchara	spoon
cucharita	teaspoon

cuchillo	knife
lista de comida	menu
plato	plate
tenedor	fork
vaso / taza	glass / cup

Tapas

albóndigas	meatballs
boquerones en vinagre	small herring in a vinegar marinade
caracoles	snails
chipirones	small squid
chorizo	paprika sausage
jamón serrano	dried ham
morcilla	blood sausage
pulpo	squid
tortilla	potato omelette

Entremeses/Starters

| aceitunas | olives |
| anchoas | anchovies |

No problems with the menu: printed menus and signs are multi-lingual

ensalada	salad
jamón	ham
mantequilla	butter
pan	bread
panecillo	bread roll
sardinas	sardines

Sopas/Soups

caldo	meat broth
gazpacho	cold vegetable soup
puchero canario	hearty soup
sopa de pescado	fish soup
sopa de verduras	vegetable soup

Platos de huevos/Egg dishes

huevo	egg
duro	hard-boiled
pasado por agua	soft-boiled
huevos a la flamenca	eggs with beans
huevos fritos	fried eggs
huevos revueltos	scrambled eggs
tortilla	omelette

Pescado/Fish

ahumado	smoked
a la plancha	grilled on a hot griddle
asado	fried
cocido	boiled
frito	baked
anguila	eel
atún	tuna
bacalao	cod
besugo	bream
lenguado	sole
merluza	hake
salmón	salmon
trucha	trout
almeja	river mussel
bogavante	lobster
calamar	squid
camarón	shrimp
cangrejo	crab

gamba	prawn
langosta	rock lobster
ostras	oysters

Carne/Meat

buey	beef
carnero	mutton
cerdo	pork
chuleta	chops
cochinillo, lechón	roast suckling pig
conejo	rabbit
cordero	lamb
ternera	veal
vaca	beef
asado	roast
bistec	beefsteak
carne ahumada	smoked meat
carne estofada	pot roast
carne salada	corned beef
fiambre	cold cuts
jamón	ham
lomo	loin or back
salchichón	hard sausage

There's lots of variety at the markets

tocino	bacon
pato	duck
pollo	chicken

Verduras/Vegetables

aceitunas	olives
cebollas	onions
col de Bruselas	Brussels sprouts
coliflor	cauliflower
espárragos	asparagus
espinacas	spinach
garbanzos	chickpeas
guisantes	peas
habas, judías	beans
lechuga	lettuce
patatas	potatoes
patatas fritas	French fries
pepinos	cucumber
tomates	tomato
zanahorias	carrots

Condimentos/Condiments

vinagre / aceite	vinegar / oil
ajo	garlic
azafrán	saffron
mostaza	mustard
sal/salado / pimienta	salt/salted / pepper

Postres/Sweets

bollo	sweet bread
dulces	sweets
flan	cream caramel
helado	ice cream
mermelada / miel	jam / honey
pastel	cake
queso	cheese
tarta	tart

Frutas/Fruit

cerezas	cherries

chumbos	prickly pears
dátiles	dates
fresas	strawberries
higos	figs
mandarinas	mandarin oranges
manzana / pera	apple / pear
melocotón	peach
melones	honeydew melon
membrillo	quince
naranjas	oranges
nueces	nuts
piña	pineapple
plátano	banana
sandías	watermelon
uvas	grape

Local Foods

bocadillo	filled roll
chorizo	red paprika sausage
churros	fried dough
migas	croutons

Beverages

agua mineral	mineral water
con/sin gas	still / sparkling
aguardiente	cordial
amontillado	medium sherry
anís	anis cordial
Brandy	brandy
cerveza	beer
café con leche	coffee with milk
café solo	espresso
café cortado	with a little milk
fino	dry sherry
leche	milk
limonada	lemonade
la Manzanilla	camomile tea
oloroso	sweet sherry
té	tea
vino	wine
blanco/tinto	white/red
rosado	rosé
dry/sweet	seco/dulce
zumo	fruit juice

Literature

A good deal of literature about many aspects of life on the Canary Islands is available in souvenir shops and bookshops on the islands themselves, but hard to get in other countries.

Jose Luis Concepcion: The Guanches: Survivors and their Descendants. Short account of the original inhabitants of the Canary Isles. The same author has written a book about the traditions of the islands entitled Costumbres, Tradiciones Canarias (available locally in English).

Florence du Cane: The Canary Isles. A.& C. Black, 1911. An entertaining view of the islands 100 years ago. Only available second-hand. *History, culture*

Felipe Fernández-Armesto: The Canary Islands After the Conquest: The Making of a Colonial Society in the Early Sixteenth Century. Clarendon Press, 1981. A scholarly work for those with a detailed interest in the subject.

José Luis Gago: Arquitecturas Contemporáneas Las Palmas de Gran Canaria 1960–2000. Excellent black-and-white photographs of interesting modern architecture in the island's capital.

José M. Castellano Gil: History of the Canary Islands. Centro de la Cultura Popular Canaria, 1993. A useful general survey.

Jose Luis Concepcion: Typical Canary Cooking; The Best Traditional Dishes, Sweets and Liquors. 1994 *Cookery*

Flora Lilia: The Best of Canarian Sauces : Mojos, Adobos, Salmorejos, Escabeches. Centro de la Cultura Popular Canaria, 2000.

Miguel Angel Cabrera Perez: Native Flora of the Canary Islands. Editorial Everest, 2000. *Nature*

Tony Clarke: A Field Guide to the Birds of the Atlantic Islands: Canary Islands, Madeira, Azores, Cape Verde. Helm Field Guides, 2006.

M.G. Sanchez and M.J.M. Valbuena: National Parks in the Canary Islands. Editorial Everest, 2001.

Noel Rochford: Landscapes of Gran Canaria. Sunflower Books, 2009. *Hiking*

Kompass »Gran Canaria« (no. 237). Map on a scale of 1 : 50 000 for walkers and mountain bikers. The one published by the National Geographical Institute (**IGN**) on Gran Canaria is even more detailed with 20 pages at 1:25 000.

Media

Foreign newspapers Foreign newspapers and magazines are available on the island the day after publication. A good range of English-language papers can be found in the tourist centres.

Local newspaper The »Island Gazette« is published in English.

Television Five Spanish-speaking TV channels can be picked up on Gran Canaria as well as satellite channels, depending on the location, including English-speaking broadcasts.

Money

Euro The euro is the official currency in Spain. Spanish coins depict Juan Carlos I (1 €, 2 €), Miguel de Cervantes (50, 20, 10 cents) and the cathedral of Santiago de Compostela (5, 2, 1 cent).

Banks Banks are open Mon–Fri 9am–2pm, Sat 9am–1pm. In the months of June to September most banks are closed on Saturdays.

ATM ATMs are available in all larger towns and have operating instructions in several languages. Money can be withdrawn using debit and credit cards with a PIN.

Credit cards Banks, larger hotels, restaurants, car rentals as well as shops accept most international credit cards like Visa, Eurocard, American Express.

▶ CONTACT DETAILS FOR CREDIT CARDS

In the event of lost bank or credit cards you can contact the following numbers in UK and USA (phone numbers when dialling from Gran Canaria):

▶ **Eurocard/MasterCard**
Tel. 001 / 636 7227 111

▶ **Visa**
Tel. 001 / 410 581 336

▶ **American Express UK**
Tel. 0044 / 1273 696 933

▶ **American Express USA**
Tel. 001 / 800 528 4800

▶ **Diners Club UK**
Tel. 0044 / 1252 513 500

▶ **Diners Club USA**
Tel. 001 / 303 799 9000
Have the bank sort code, account number and card number as well as the expiry date ready.
The following numbers of UK banks (dialling from Gran Canaria) can be used to report and

cancel lost or stolen bank and credit cards issued by those banks:

► **NatWest**
Tel. 0044 / 142 370 0545

► **HSBC**
Tel. 0044 / 1442 422 929

► **Lloyds TSB**
Tel. 0044 / 1702 278 270

► **Barclaycard**
Tel. 0044 / 1604 230 230

Post · Communications

Postcards and letters are automatically sent by **airmail** and generally take five days to central Europe. Postage for postcards (postales) and letters (cartas) up to 20 grams within Europe costs 0.53 €. Large postcards cost 1.03 €. Stamps (sellos) can be bought where you buy the postcards or at the post office. The mailboxes are yellow.

Letters

Fax messages can be sent from post offices (Correos); **phone cards** are also available, but it is not possible to telephone from the post office. Post offices are open Mon–Fri 9am–2pm, Sat 9am–1pm.

Post offices

Phone calls to other countries can be made from public telephone booths using coins or a telephone card (tarjeta telefónica). Telephone cards can be bought in tobacco shops, kiosks and at the post office. Phone calls from hotels and holiday apartments can be up to three times as expensive as from public phones. Telephone rates are much cheaper on Saturday afternoons, Sundays and at night.

Telephone

The system used on the Canary Isles, GSM 900/1800, is compatible with European mobile phones but not with most North American phones.

◄ Mobile telephones

Spanish telephone numbers have nine digits. They begin with the area code (for Gran Canaria, Fuerteventura and Lanzarote: **928**), which must be dialled when making local calls as well. The western Canary Islands (Tenerife, La Gomera, La Palma and El Hierro) have the area code 922.

Telephone numbers

▶ AREA CODES

TO SPAIN

To Gran Canaria: 0034

FROM GRAN CANARIA

To Australia: tel. 0061

To the Republic of Ireland:
tel. 00353
To UK: 0044
To USA and Canada: 001

Prices

Tips Generally a service charge is included in the bill; but hotel employees, waiters, taxi drivers etc. expect an additional tip of about 5–10% of the bill. We recommend giving the hotel maid her first tip on the day after you arrive and then once a week; they get 3–5 € per week.

 WHAT DOES IT COST?

Three-course menu
From €25

Simple meal
From €6

Cup of coffee
€2

Short bus journey
From €1.50

Basic double room
From €50

Glass of beer
€2.50

Security

As **theft** is common in the large tourist centres, it is better to leave valuables and personal documents in the hotel safe or hotel room safe. Never leave anything in a rental car. Keep the car doors and boot locked when driving: in Las Palmas young people who offer their services as »window cleaners« at traffic lights often use the opportunity to steal items from cars.

Shopping

Free trade zone The Canary Islands have been a free trade zone since 1852. However, the lack of customs duty does not necessarily mean that prices are low, although tobacco products, spirits and perfume products are cheaper than at home.

Shopping centres There are huge shopping centres with supermarkets, boutiques and many small shops in the tourist centres in the south. The largest selection by far is in **Las Palmas**. While the shops line up in the pedestrian zone Calle Triana, in Avenida Mesa y López there are department stores to explore.

Most shops are open Mon–Fri 9am–1pm and 4pm–8pm, Sat 9am–1pm. In the tourist centres some shops open longer, and even on Sundays.

Hours

Timples (small stringed instruments) are typical of the Canaries. The best **needlework** comes from Ingenio, where drawn-work embroidery (»calados«) – table cloths, blouses, aprons etc. – is made in a school for craftwork (with salesroom). The pretty **pottery and ceramic wares** are in part still made in the traditional way without a potter's wheel. **Basketry** made from palm leaves, reeds and willow is available everywhere. Seeds or shoots from local plants or a bouquet of **bird of paradise flowers**, which are packed by the florists for travel, are an attractive souvenir from the Canary Islands. Alcoholic souvenirs include Canarian wine and **banana cordial**.

Crafts and souvenirs

> ### _i_ Interesting markets
>
> - Puerto de Mogán: the Friday market around the harbour attracts many tourists.
> - Teror: fresh produce and groceries of all kinds and crafts at weekends. Don't miss the crusty bread.
> - Mercado de las Palmas in the Vegueta: huge selection of fresh fruit and vegetables, fish, meat, cheese (daily except Sundays)
> - Las Palmas: large Sunday flea market at Mercado del Puerto

Sports and Outdoors

Hiking, biking, golf, diving, surfing – Gran Canaria is a paradise for sports lovers with an unbelievably varied and large selection. There is hardly a four- or five-star hotel that does not have tennis courts and a gym.

In a short time Gran Canaria has been developed into a golfer's paradise. The island now has seven golf courses and more are being built.

Golf

Cycling on Gran Canaria is something for fit people. Bear in mind that the island has no bike paths, the winds are often strong and the weather is hot. There are sharp stones that could puncture tyres on the trails in the interior. Mountain bikes are best suited for biking on Gran Canaria.

Cycling

There are several riding stables on Gran Canaria that rent to tourists, offer riding lessons or organize trips on horseback.

Horseback riding

JUST DON'T HURT HIM ...!

Almost every town of any size on Gran Canaria has fields where »lucha canaria« (Canarian wrestling) matches are held. Another less well-known Canarian sport is »juego del palo« (stick fight).

The two »pollos« (fighting cocks) take their starting position. Each bends forward, places his right foot slightly forward and bends his legs while grabbing the rolled up trouser leg of his opponent with his left hand. At the same time the two participants shake hands with their right hands. Then the referee gives the signal and the fight begins. Manolo grabs his opponent, the tanned Antonio, by the rolled-up pants and tries to throw him to the ground over his hip. But Antonio has seen through it and is able to resist this hip throw. The two men gasp, stamp their feet, pull and grab each other. Then Antonio grabs his opponent's shirt with his right hand and pulls Manolo towards himself; he lifts him up and throws him with a loud shout over his left shoulder. Manolo lands with a dull thud on his back on the black sand. The point goes to Antonio.

Wrestling Canary-Style

Some historians presume that Canarian wrestling originated in ancient Egypt. Others think that »lucha canaria« was invented by the ancient Canarians. In the 15th century the Spanish chronicler Alvar Garcia de Santa Maria reported that wrestling was very popular among the early Canarians as a noble and chivalrous kind of martial art. Its primary aim was not to defeat the opponent but to make up after the match with a peaceful embrace. »Lucha canaria« is still very popular on the Canaries, taking second place after football. There are wrestling clubs and grounds in every sizeable town, and matches are held regularly. The tournament rules made in 1872 are still in use. Thus only two teams compete against each other, each team consisting of twelve wrestlers (recently including women), of which each member of

»Lucha canaria« is very popular on Gran Canaria. The best wrestlers are treated like stars with the status of football or tennis stars in other countries.

each team wrestles against one member of the opposing team. The barefoot wrestlers wear sturdy shirts and pants that have been rolled up over the knees. The opposing »luchador« has to be thrown within two minutes. To do this almost everything is allowed: the wrestlers may push, pull, yank, lift or throw; hitting, kicking, punching, twisting and painful grips are not allowed. Only the body can be attacked, never the head. Each match lasts three rounds, and the winner is the one who throws his opponent twice. The winner then wrestles the winner of another match, and can only wrestle three other opponents after his first one. The team that gets twelve points with a two-point lead over the other team in the two-hour tournament is the winner. Incidentally, it is considered to be good sportsmanship for the winners to say at the end that the other team won.

A Matter of Agility

Another less well-known Canarian sport is »juego del palo«, a stick fight or stick fencing. Here two opponents simulate attack and defence with a 2.5cm/1in-thick, shoulder-high stick (palo), which they grip with both hands. Real experts can judge the simulated hits, thrusts and stabs, which are made with minimum physical effort, so well that they stop only millimetres from the opponent's body. The worst thing that can happen to a duellist is to lose his stick. This guarantees dishonour and shame. Before the Spanish conquest of the Canaries the stick fights were part of a dangerous duel, for example between the chiefs of opposing tribes. The Spanish quickly prohibited the Canarians from carrying arms. It was only at the end of the Franco era in 1975 that the Canarians became more conscious of their own native ancestry, history and culture, and thus resurrected stick fighting. The winner of the »juego del palo« is chosen by intuition. What matters is not winning, but the elegance of movement and adherence to rules and rituals.

Sailing, windsurfing

Winds are strong along some parts of the coast; beginners might not find the sailing easy here. Sailors and windsurfers find ideal conditions on the south and south-west coast of Gran Canaria.

Sailing lessons are given in Puerto Rico. Surfboards can be rented in Playa del Inglés, San Agustín, Puerto de Mogán and Puerto Rico. The surfing for experienced windsurfers is at Pozo Izquierdo near El Doctoral. Beginners find suitable conditions in the summer in Bahía Feliz and Playa del Aguila.

Diving

Diving conditions around the Canary Islands are ideal. There are ten diving schools on Gran Canaria, most of them in the south or south-west of the island. They offer beginners' and advanced courses in many of the hotels. They also organize diving trips to the underwater park at Arinaga with its beautiful sea flora and fauna.

Many large hotels have excellent **tennis courts**, most of them with floodlights. There are usually tennis teachers available. Some hotels offer tennis holidays as a package.

Baedeker TIP

Water sports with a difference

Puerto Rico is the centre for water sports on the island. Sailing and surfing are on offer, of course, but as an alternative how about a banana boat ride or jet skis? Paragliding over the water is also a favourite activity. Information on the beach at Puerto Rico.

Waterskiing

Waterskiing is offered at Playa del Inglés, in the Aquamarina (between Arguineguín and Puerto Rico) and in Puerto Rico.

Hiking

Thanks to its varied landscape, lush vegetation and excellent climate the island's interior is ideal for hiking. Various hiking tours are described in the section »Sights from A to Z«. ▶Barrancos von Agaete, Arguineguín and Guayadeque are especially suited for hiking. A walk around ▶ Caldera de Bandama is not difficult. The ▶ Roque Nublo and Roque Bentaiga (▶ Tejeda) can easily be climbed even without mountain climbing experience. ▶ Fataga and Mogán are also good starting points for a tour. Anyone who wants to combine swimming and hiking should follow the route to Playa de Güigüí (▶Baedeker Special, p. 192). Trails on Gran Canaria are not signposted. A good **hiking guidebook** and hiking map (▶Literature) are very helpful.

Every Sunday the **group »Montañero«** offers a **guided hike**. The tours are usually between 12 and 20km (7–12mi) long and of varying degrees of difficulty. A picnic is included. The group meets at the Mobil petrol station in Arguineguín (8am); participants pay a small fee to cover expenses (information at the tourist office in Playa del Inglés under Tel. 928 77 65 02).

Deep-sea fishing

Ideal conditions for deep-sea fishing can be found just two miles off the coast of Gran Canaria. Boats start regularly especially from Puerto Rico and Puerto de Mogán; previous experience is not necessary.

INFORMATION SPORTS AND OUTDOORS

CYCLING

Both of these agencies rent mountain bikes and other bikes, and organize guided tours of varying degrees of difficulty.

► **Happy Biking**
Hotel IFA Continental
Avenida Italia 2
Playa del Inglés
Tel. 928 76 68 32, fax 928 76 68 43
www.happy-biking.com

► **Free Motion**
Hotel Sandy Beach
Avenida Alfereces Provisionales
Playa del Inglés
Tel. 928 77 74 79, fax 928 77 52 99
www.free-motion.net
Guided mountain hiking tours
from easy to difficult; a day tour including transfer and Nordic walking sticks costs about 40 €.
Introductory Nordic walking courses are also offered.

DIVING

► **Diving Center Nautico**
In the IFA Interclub Atlantic
Los Jazmines 2, San Agustín
Tel. 928 77 81 68
www.divers-web.de
The diving centre offers an extensive selection of courses, from introductory courses to underwater photo safaris.

The mountains in the interior are a challenge for mountain bikers

A well-earned rest: hikers above San Nicolás de Tolentino

▶ **Sun Sub**
In Hotel Buenaventura Playa
Plaza de Ansite s/n
Playa del Inglés
Tel. 928 77 81 65
www.sunsub.com
The courses for children and
teenagers are organized according
to age groups. Most of the diving
is done on the reef off Pasito
Blanco.

▶ **Top Diving**
Puerto Escala, Puerto Rico
Tel. 928 56 06 09
www.topdiving.net
Boats take divers to sites including
the wrecks off Puerto de Mogán.

GOLF

▶ **Real Club de Golf Las Palmas**
Carretera de Bandama s/n
Las Palmas
Tel. 928 35 01 04, fax 928 35 01 10
www.realclubdegolf
delaspalmas.com

18-hole golf course in the club
founded in 1891. Wonderful views.

▶ **El Cortijo Club de Campo**
Autopista del Sur
km 6.4 near Telde
Tel. 928 71 11 11
Fax 928 71 49 05
www.elcortijo.es
18-hole course with very old palm
trees.

▶ **El Cortijo Golf Center**
Right next to the El Cortijo Club
Tel. 928 68 48 90, fax 928 68 29 40
E-Mail: nisular@vodafone.es
Relatively small 18-hole course
and the only course on the island
with floodlights so that it can be
used at night.

▶ **Club de Golf Maspalomas**
Avda. T.O. Neckermann s/n
Maspalomas
Tel. 928 76 25 81, fax 928 76 82 45
www.maspalomasgolf.net

This 18-hole course is located in the dunes of Maspalomas near the ocean.

▶ Salobre Golf & Resort

Autopista Gran Canaria 1, km 53
Urb. El Salobre / Maspalomas
Tel. 928 01 01 03
Fax 928 01 01 04
www.salobregolfresort.com
18-hole course with a view of the mountains and the sea. In 2004 a 9-hole golf course was opened next to it, which is now being expanded to 18 holes.

▶ Anfi Tauro Golf

Barranco del Lechugal
Valle de Tauro s/n
Mogán
Tel. 928 12 88 40 / 41
Fax 928 56 03 42
www.anfitauro.es
A 9-hole course with beautiful lakes. In 2005 another 9-hole course was opened next to it, which is also being expanded to 18 holes.

RIDING

▶ Real Club de Golf

Carretera de Bandama s/n
Tel. 928 35 19 0

▶ Black Horse

El Salobre 66
El Tablero
Tel. 928 14 23 94

TENNIS

▶ Tennis Center Maspalomas

Avenida Touroperador
Tjaereborg 9
Tel. 928 76 74 47
Tennis and squash are available on public sand and hard courts.

WINDSURFING

▶ Club Mistral

Autopista del Sur, km 44
Bahía Feliz
Tel. 928 15 71 58
www.club-mistral.com/
grancanaria
The well-known surfing centre on the beach of Bahía Feliz offers courses for beginners and advanced divers. They also organize trips for divers to the nearby Pozo de Izquierdo known for its strong winds.

▶ Side Shore (Dunkerbeck's Windsurf Center)

Plaza de Hibiscos 1
Playa del Aguila
Tel. 928 76 29 58
www.sideshore-es.com

Time

The Canary Islands are in the **Western European Time zone** (WET), two hours ahead of Greenwich Mean Time. As European summer time is used from April to October, the time difference to other parts of Europe is constant all year round.

Since the archipelago is so close to the equator the number of daylight hours does not vary as much between summer and winter on the Canaries as in northern Europe: The longest summer day has about 14 hours of daylight, the shortest winter day about 11 hours.

Transport

Driving

The Canarians drive **on the right**, just like on the Spanish mainland and the rest of continental Europe.

Speed limits: within towns the speed limit is 50km/h (30mph); outside towns it is 90km/h (55mph), on motorways 100km/h (60mph).

Right of way goes to the car approaching from the right (exceptions are marked). In **roundabouts** the car within the roundabout has the right of way.

On some main roads in order to **turn left** it is necessary to exit right into a small roundabout and then cross the main road. Foreigners often do not understand this rule, thereby causing serious accidents. Watch out for traffic signs that are placed in the middle of the road.

If the street is well-lit (except for four-lane roads and motorways) driving **with parking lights is allowed**; watch out for cars without lights!

When passing be sure to blink left first and then right, and to leave the blinker on until passing is complete. Honking is required when passing and before entering a curve (flashing lights in the dark). **Passing is not allowed** 100m/110yd before the crest of a hill as well as on roads with less than 200m/220yd visibility.

Seatbelts are required in the front and back seats when driving.

The limit for alcohol is **0.5 per mille**.

Towing by private vehicles is not allowed. In case of an **accident** – no matter who is at fault – expect the car to be confiscated (it will be released after the trial); in case of a serious accident the driver might even be arrested. After every accident get in touch with the Spanish insurance company listed on the International Green Insurance Card so that payment of a deposit, if required, can be arranged. If the car is rented the rental papers will explain what to do in case of an accident.

Rental cars

The best way to explore the island is with a rental car. There are rental agencies (alquiler de coches) in all tourist centres. It is practical to rent the car at home and collect it from the airport when you arrive. Car hire is cheap on the Canary Isles in comparison to most European countries. A car in the lowest category costs between 20 and 30 € per day at international rental agencies, depending on the length

▶ ADDRESSES

AUTOMOBILE CLUB / TOWING SERVICE

▶ **Real Automóvil Club de Gran Canaria**
Calle León y Castillo 279
Las Palmas
Tel. 928 23 07 88
Towing service:
Tel. 902 30 05 05

If you are driving a rental car it is best to contact the agency. If the breakdown involves your own car the police (tel. 112) will also help.

CAR RENTALS

▶ **Avis**
Tel. 902 18 08 54
www.avis.com

▶ **Europcar**
Tel. 922 37 28 56
www.europcar.com

▶ **Hertz**
Tel. 901 10 07 77
www.hertz.com

BUS

▶ **Global**
Playa del Inglés
Yumbo Shopping Centre
Tel. 9 28 76 53 32
Hours: Mon–Fri 9am–1.30pm and 3.30pm–6pm

Las Palmas: Estación de Guaguas
Avenida Rafael Cabrera
Tel. 928 36 83 35
Hours: daily 6am–10pm
www.globalsu.net

▶ **Useful routes**
Line 30: Las Palmas – Maspalomas
(7am–8pm every 20 min. express)
Line 5: Las Palmas–Maspalomas
(8pm–7am hourly)
Line 1: Las Palmas–Puerto Mogán
Line 60: Airport–Las Palmas

AIR TRAFFIC

▶ **Airport information**
Aeropuerto de Gando
Tel. 928 25 41 40

▶ **Binter Canarias**
Aeropuerto de Gando
Tel. 928 57 99 33
Central reservations:
tel. 902 39 13 92
www.bintercanarias.com

SHIPPING COMPANIES

▶ **Líneas Fred. Olsen**
Puerto de las Nieves harbour
Tel. 928 55 42 62
Central reservations:
Tel. 902 10 01 07
www.fredolsen.es

▶ **Naviera Armas**
Calle Doctor Juan Dominguez
Pérez 2
Las Palmas
Tel. 902 45 65 00
www.navieraarmas.com

▶ **Trasmediterránea**
Plaza Mr. Jolly s/n
Las Palmas
Tel. 928 47 41 21
www.trasmediterranea.com

TAXI

Las Palmas:
Tel. 928 46 22 12
Maspalomas:
Tel. 928 76 67 67
Playa del Inglés:
Tel. 928 14 26 34
Puerto Rico:
Tel. 928 56 18 76

of the rental. Rental contracts are generally made with unlimited mileage. Comprehensive insurance is recommended and costs about 3 € extra per day (damage to tyres when driving on unpaved roads is not covered). Smaller companies are generally cheaper. A **credit card** is absolutely necessary.

Taxis

Taxi drivers are required to use the meter at all times. The charges run about 1.00 € per kilometre. Trips at night and baggage cost extra. Waiting is also charged.

Bus transport

All towns are served by bus lines. Global runs 312 buses on 119 routes and serves more than 2400 bus stops on the island. Bus stops marked with a »P« (parada) have schedules posted (horarios); tickets can be bought from the driver. Schedules can also be picked up in the Global offices and at tourist centres.

Transport in Las Palmas ▶

In Las Palmas there are three bus lines with yellow buses (Guaguas Municipales). The main bus terminal is at Avenida Rafael Cabrera near Parque San Telmo; the routes end at Avenida Primero de Mayo, Plaza Cairasco and Teatro Pérez.

Ferries

All islands are served regularly by the Spanish state-owned shipping company Compañía Trasmediterránea or by the operators Fred. Olsen and Naviera Armas.

Gran Canaria – Tenerife ▶

Trasmediterránea ferries run from Las Palmas to **Santa Cruz de Tenerife**; the trip takes about 4 hours and costs about 40 € per person. The jetfoil (Mon–Sat 5 times a day, Sun 3 times a day) also runs on this route. It only takes 80 minutes (only passengers; costs about twice as much as the ferry).
From **Agaete** (Puerto de las Nieves) Lineas Fred. Olsen car and passenger ferries run up to eight times a day to Santa Cruz de Tenerife (prices comparable to Las Palmas; duration: 1 hour). From Las Palmas there is a free bus to Agaete (departure: Parque de Santa Catali-

Canary Islands *Travel routes*

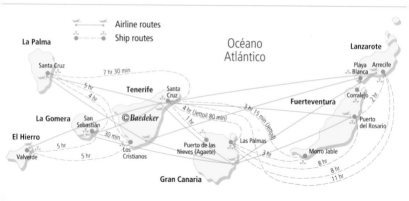

na, 60 minutes before the ferry leaves); from Agaete buses depart for Las Palmas 15 minutes after the ferry arrives.

Trasmediterránea runs a jetfoil from Las Palmas to **Morro Jable** (approx. 90 minutes, only passengers). Car ferries also depart from here daily and take about 4 hours. Trasmediterránea runs to **Puerto del Rosario** 3 times a week, Naviera Armas 4 times a week (duration approx. 8 hours).

◀ Gran Canaria – Fuerteventura

Both Trasmediterránea (3 times a week) and Naviera Armas (6 times a week) operate car ferries from Las Palmas to **Arrecife** on Lanzarote.

◀ Gran Canaria – Lanzarote

From Gran Canaria to the western part of the archipelago (La Gomera, La Palma, El Hierro) by ferry, change in Santa Cruz de Tenerife.

◀ To the western Canaries

From Puerto Rico in southern Gran Canaria boats run several times a day to the nearby tourist centres Arguineguín and Puerto de Mogán (passengers only).

◀ Ship transport from Puerto Rico

All flights from and to Gran Canaria depart and arrive at Aeropuerto de Gando. It is located about 22km/13mi south of Las Palmas.

Air transport

Binter Canarias flies from Aeropuerto de Gando several times a day to Fuerteventura, Lanzarote, Tenerife (north and south airport), La Palma and La Gomera, to El Hierro several times a week. Flying times are between 25 and 50 minutes. **Early reservations** are recommended, especially before holidays; this applies above all to the smaller islands. Overweight luggage is charged at a minimal rate or not at all.

◀ Flights between the islands

When to Go

The Canaries are often called the »islands of eternal spring«. This cliché comes from a climate that is much the same all year round (▶ p.30). Temperatures vary no more than 6°C/10°F between the cold and warm months. This makes the islands a popular destination in the **winter** for sun-starved Europeans. As far as the vegetation goes, March is an especially suitable time, when everything is in full bloom.

While in winter rooms are only available with reservations far in advance, in the **summer months** many hotels are not full, even though the climate is then still very pleasant on Gran Canaria: there are few hot and humid days.

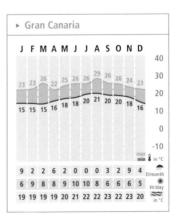

▶ Gran Canaria

	J	F	M	A	M	J	J	A	S	O	N	D	
													40
	23	23	22	25	26	26	29	26	24	23			30
													20
	15	15	15	16	18	18	20	21	20	18	16		10
													0
													-10
max min													☀ in °C
	9	2	2	6	2	0	0	0	3	2	9	4	☁ D/month
	6	9	8	8	9	10	10	8	6	6	6	5	☀ Hr/day
	19	19	19	19	20	21	22	22	23	22	23	20	≈ in °C

Tours

OUR TOURS TAKE YOU TO
THE NATURAL AND CULTURAL
HIGHLIGHTS OF THE ISLAND –
LIKE BARRANCO DE AGAETE ON
THIS PAGE – AND SHOW YOU THE
BEST PLACES TO TAKE A BREAK.

TOURS ON GRAN CANARIA

All but one of these routes through the island's most beautiful towns and natural landscape begin in the tourist centres on the Costa Canaria. All are day trips and include recommendations on where to eat and take breaks en route.

━━━ TOUR 1 Around the island
Gran Canaria is not large – it is possible to drive around the island in one day. But this doesn't leave much time for more than a quick stop at the various sights. ▶ **page 109**

━━━ TOUR 2 Fascinating mountain scenery
The most beautiful spots in the »other« Gran Canaria away from the beaches and tourist centres can be seen on this tour. ▶ **page 112**

━━━ TOUR 3 Through the south on the trail of the Guanches
This route introduces the culture of the ancient inhabitants of the Canary Islands and includes the south of Gran Canaria with its deep barrancos. ▶ **page 114**

━━━ TOUR 4 Highlights in the north
Those familiar with the south of the island will be surprised at the lush green of the north. Take this tour on Sunday in order to visit the local markets. ▶ **page 116**

━━━ TOUR 5 By Jeep into lonely country
Even if the roads have improved considerably, this tour into the interior always includes a touch of adventure. ▶ **page 118**

✳ Puerto de las Nieves

✳ Agaete

TOUR 1 ✳ Pinar de Tamadaba

Mirador de Balcón

TOUR 5

San Nicolás de Tolentino

✳ Barranco de la Aldea

©Baedeker

● Mogán

TOUR 1

✳✳ Puerto de Mogán

Puerto Rico

Puerto Rico
The spectacular water and swimming complex makes this tourist centre all the more popular

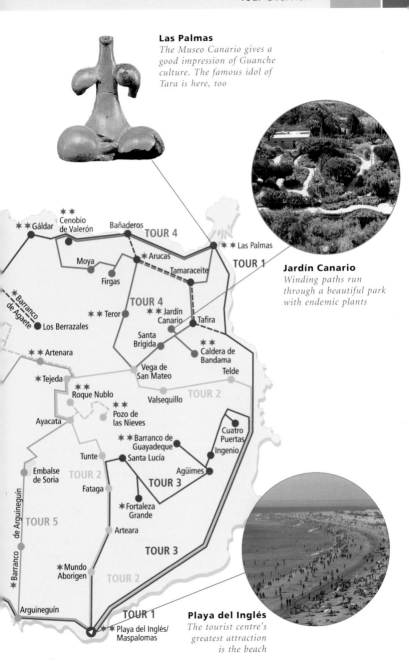

Las Palmas
The Museo Canario gives a good impression of Guanche culture. The famous idol of Tara is here, too

Jardín Canario
Winding paths run through a beautiful park with endemic plants

Gáldar
Cenobio de Valerón
Bañaderos
TOUR 4
Las Palmas
TOUR 1
Moya
Arucas
Tamaraceite
Firgas
Barranco de Agaete
TOUR 4
Teror
Los Berrazales
Jardín Canario
Tafira
Santa Brígida
Artenara
Caldera de Bandama
Tejeda
Vega de San Mateo
Telde
Roque Nublo
Valsequillo
TOUR 2
Pozo de las Nieves
Ayacata
Barranco de Guayadeque
Cuatro Puertas
Tunte
Santa Lucía
Ingenio
Embalse de Soria
Agüimes
Fataga
TOUR 2
TOUR 3
Barranco de Arguineguín
Fortaleza Grande
TOUR 5
Arteara
TOUR 3
Mundo Aborigen
TOUR 2
Arguineguín
TOUR 1
Playa del Inglés/Maspalomas

Playa del Inglés
The tourist centre's greatest attraction is the beach

Holiday on Gran Canaria

The right place for a holiday
Most guests come for the sun and sand. They find this most often in the south and south-west, which, unlike the more cloudy north, are ideal for swimming all year round. By far the largest tourist centres are **Costa Canaria**, known for the holiday resorts Playa del Inglés, Maspalomas and San Agustín, and **Costa Mogán** between Arguineguín and Puerto de Mogán. But don't expect to find island culture here, since almost all the holiday resorts in the south only sprang up as part of the tourism boom of the last 40 years.

Costa Canaria ▶
If you are not bothered by an artificial-looking resort, you will enjoy **Playa del Inglés**. Miles-long beaches, a large selection of sports and other activities as well as a variety of great nightlife are the main attractions of this holiday resort. The nearby **Maspalomas** and the new town **Costa Meloneras** to the west are more luxurious. The exclusive hotels and comfortable bungalow villages are not as close together; they are a good choice for people looking for peace and quiet. **San Agustín** east of Playa del Inglés is also more tranquil. Many of the hotels here are not new and the beach is not as wide either, but San Agustín lives from loyal guests who do not need the best of everything when on holiday. **Playa de Aguila** and **Bahía Feliz** on the edge of San Agustín attract young surfers.

Costa Mogán ▶
The largest and most popular tourist site on Costa Mogán is **Puerto Rico**. Not everyone likes the hive-like apartment complexes that stretch up the cliffs, but the area is spoilt for sunshine and the sheltered location make the harbour the largest centre for water sports in the Canary Islands. The relatively small beach, however, cannot keep up with the tourist crowds in the high season. The nearby **Playa de los Amadores**, where several luxury resorts were built recently, relieves the congestion. Of the resorts north-west of Puerto Rico, **Puerto de Mogán** is considered to be one of the most successful examples of holiday architecture. The area around the yacht harbour is a beautiful place to stay but the »Venice of Gran Canaria« is generally flooded by day-trippers.

Las Palmas ▶
Anyone looking for local Canarian and Spanish culture will find it in the capital city of Las Palmas. The city has an excellent public beach and a large selection of hotels in all categories, but is not very quiet. The colonial old quarter with its interesting museums, attractive festivals and its carnival has a broad selection of culture and entertainment.

Turismo Rural ▶
The mountains offer holidays of a different kind. Rural tourism (Turismo Rural) is a movement that has restored country estates and hotels in the interior; these are ideal bases for nature-loving guests

and hikers who want to discover the breathtaking mountains and lakes. This is the right place to spend the nicest weeks of the year away from crowds (see Baedeker Tip, p.127).

The public **bus network** on Gran Canaria is excellent. Buses from Costa Canaria and Las Palmas run to many of the attractions and make day trips possible. But in order to explore the more remote west coast and the central mountains a **rental car** is necessary. The roads along the coast are excellent except in the west and there is a motorway from the capital to the holiday resorts in the south. But the mountain roads in the interior are narrow and winding, and best left to experienced drivers. 4-wheel-drive vehicles are necessary for off-road tours.

The right means of transport

Tour 1 Around the island

Start and finish: Playa del Inglés   **Duration:** 1 day
Length: 212km/127mi

This drive around the island is almost a must for first-time visitors to Gran Canaria, for it gives a wonderful impression of the island's varied landscape. Of course, there is little time to tour the individual attractions at length.

Leave ❶**Playa del Inglés** or Maspalomas heading west. Pass the fishing village of Arguineguín on a good coastal road to ❷**Puerto Rico** with its artificial beach. The western point of the large tourist region in southern Gran Canaria is ❸✳✳ **Puerto de Mogán**. A stroll through Gran Canaria's »Little Venice« is a must! The coastal road ends in Puerto de Mogán. Continue on the road GC 200 northwards through the fertile Barranco de Mogán. On both sides of the road small houses with gardens cling to the slopes of the mountains. Another 8km/5mi from Puerto de Mogán lies the town of ❹**Mogán**.
The main road now runs north-west and begins to climb. Vegetation becomes sparse. About 10km/6mi beyond Mogán a rock wall on the right shimmers in many colours. It is called Azulejos. After a further 8km/5mi, the old pass road to Degollada de Tasártico leads off to the left. Since there is not much to see on the old road, it is better to continue on the GC 200.
From Tocodomán the area is again populated and the plains with alluvial land and an ample water supply around ❺**San Nicolás de Tolentino** have the right conditions for productive agriculture. There are windmills to pump the water to the surface, but since the underground water table is sinking not many of them are still running. For a long time San Nicolás de Tolentino's only contact with the out-

side world went through Puerto de la Aldea. Beyond this little port the GC 200 runs mostly along the coast again.

The main road offers several magnificent views; a stop at ❻ **Mirador de Balcón** is a must. Along this part of Gran Canaria's coast there are steep cliffs to the ocean and countless curves along the 40km/25mi from San Nicolás de Tolentino to ❼ ✳ **Agaete**.

Side trip to Barranco de Agaete

The town is located at the mouth of the ❽ ✳ **Barranco de Agaete** and is considered to be the most fertile part of the island. A drive to the former spa Los Berrazales (8km/5mi one way) goes through lush tropical and subtropical vegetation; coffee is even grown here.

✔ **DON'T MISS**

- Stroll through Puerto de Mogán, Gran Canaria's »Little Venice«
- Enjoy the view at Mirador de Balcón
- Lunch and a swim in Puerto de las Nieves
- Tour of the mysterious Cenobio de Valerón
- Shopping and dinner in the capital city

In the centre of Agaete a road turns off westwards to ❾ ✳ **Puerto de las Nieves** (1km/0.5mi); from here there is an excellent view of the bizarre rock Dedo de Dios and many excellent restaurants where local fish can be tasted. Leave Agaete on the GC 2 to the north-east and after 5km/3mi on the right side are the Cueva de las Cruces, several tiny caves. Shortly after, a road leads off to the left to Sardina and a small reptile park (Reptilandia). Those who continue on the main road will reach ❿ ✳✳ **Gáldar** after 4km/2.5mi. Stop here for a stroll through a typical Canary Island town.

Side trip to La Guancha

Gáldar was already settled in pre-Spanish times, as the housing remains and graves of La Guancha show. It is located 2km/1¼mi north of Gáldar near the town of El Agujero. There is a signposted road on the western edge of Gáldar and a sign at the church in Gáldar to El Agujero.

Gáldar and the town of Santa María de Guía, 2km/1¼mi to the east, have practically merged. Guía, as it is called for short, lives mainly from bananas. Just beyond Guía leave the GC 2 and continue the trip around the island on the winding old coastal road. This road leads to ⓫ ✳✳ **Cenobio de Valerón**, one of the most interesting early Canarian sites. The mountain with its cave complex offers a fantastic view of the Cuesta de Silva coastline.

The region was named after Diego de Silva, who tried to land here during the Spanish conquest in the 15th century. The old coastal road winds along the mountain slopes and meets a more modern road at San Felipe. The cliffs are less steep here than in western Gran Canaria and there are only a few pebble or sand coves. The fertile land in the delta of the barrancos is mainly used to cultivate bananas.

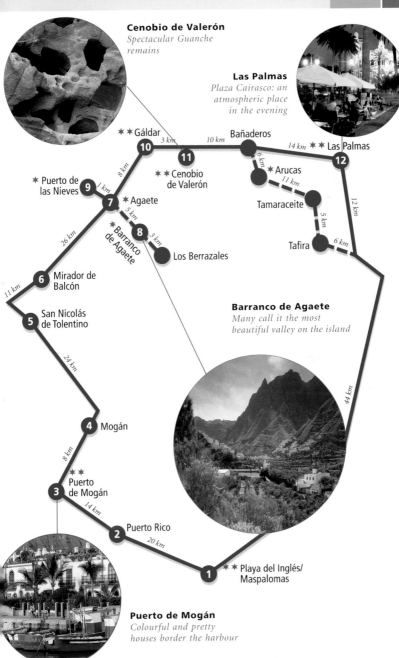

Cenobio de Valerón
Spectacular Guanche remains

Las Palmas
Plaza Cairasco: an atmospheric place in the evening

** **Gáldar**   3 km   Bañaderos   14 km ** **Las Palmas**
10   **11**   **12**

8 km   6 km   * **Arucas**
                                              11 km

* **Puerto de** **9** 1 km   **Tamaraceite**
las Nieves   **7**   * **Agaete**   5 km
                   5 km   **Tafira**   6 km
26 km   **8**   * **Barranco**
                 3 km   de Agaete
                         ** **Cenobio**
                         de Valerón
                                    Los Berrazales

6 Mirador de
       Balcón

11 km   12 km

5 San Nicolás
       de Tolentino

24 km

Barranco de Agaete
Many call it the most beautiful valley on the island

4 Mogán   44 km

8 km

** **
3 Puerto
de Mogán

14 km

2 Puerto Rico
              20 km

              1 ** **Playa del Inglés/**
                         Maspalomas

Puerto de Mogán
Colourful and pretty houses border the harbour

Alternative route via Arucas and Tafira

For those who do not want to stop in Las Palmas on this tour we recommend turning off the east-west route at Bañaderos to avoid the chaotic traffic of the capital and to enjoy the beautiful landscape on this alternative route. Arucas with its huge neo-Gothic church, Tamaraceite and Tafira (where the Jardín Canario is worth a visit for an impression of the overwhelming variety of plant life on the Canary Islands) finally lead to Marzagán. From there the motorway is a quick connection to the south of the island.

Main route via Las Palmas

The coastal road to the north reveals the less pleasant side of the city. There are industrial sites and poorer residential areas along the coast, but the centre of ⑫✱✱ **Las Palmas** makes a different impression. The many attractions and opportunities to shop make it an inviting place to stop. One of the good restaurants in the island capital is an ideal place to end the day. In southern Las Palmas, in the old quarter of Vegueta, the motorway begins and leads back to the tourist centres in the south.

Tour 2 Fascinating mountain scenery

Start and finish: Playa del Inglés
Length: 130km/78mi

Duration: at least 6 hours

This route to the central mountains is without question the most beautiful on Gran Canaria. In order to see as much as possible of the landscape, make the trip in good weather. It pays to start early to beat the clouds that form due to the trade winds.

Leave ①**Playa del Inglés** via the suburb of San Fernando and follow the signs northwards to Tunte or San Bartolomé de Tirajana. You will soon leave the houses behind and be captivated by the mountains. There are constantly changing views of the barren and bizarre landscape. After 6km/3.5mi a stop at ②✱ **Mundo Aborigen** is worthwhile; it is a theme park on the early Canarian peoples. The first town, ③**Arteara**, appears after 10km/6mi. The countryside gradually gets greener; there are small oases, palm trees and occasional lemon or orange groves. There is a camel safari here as well as a new and very informative archaeological park on the Guanches. The road continues north and soon the first houses of ④**Fataga** appear. The town is picturesque with its many palm trees. 8km/5mi north of Fataga lies ⑤**Tunte** (San Barto-

DON'T MISS

- A stop at the palm tree oasis of Fataga
- A short hike to Roque Nublo
- The view from Pozo de las Nieves
- A midday stop at one of the cave restaurants in Artenara
- A tour of the church of Telde

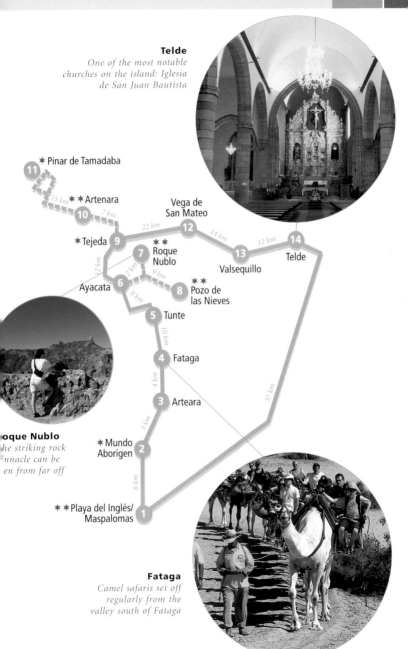

Telde
*One of the most notable
churches on the island: Iglesia
de San Juan Bautista*

11 ✷ Pinar de Tamadaba

15 km ✷✷ Artenara

10 7 km

Vega de
San Mateo

✷ Tejeda **9** 22 km **12** 14 km **13** 12 km **14**

12 km ✷✷
7 Roque
Nublo

Telde

6 2 km 9 km **8** ✷✷ Valsequillo

Ayacata Pozo de
las Nieves

8 km

5 Tunte

10 km

4 Fataga

4 km

3 Arteara

5 km

✷ Mundo
Aborigen

2

6 km

✷✷ Playa del Inglés/
Maspalomas **1**

37 km

oque Nublo
*he striking rock
*nnacle can be
en from far off

Fataga
*Camel safaris set off
regularly from the
valley south of Fataga*

lomé de Tirajana), the administrative centre for southern Gran Canaria. The area is agricultural and the major crops are varieties of fruit. The fruit is mainly used to produce liqueurs and cordials. About 10km/6mi beyond Tunte is the tiny village of ⑥**Ayacata**.

Side trip to Roque Nublo and Pozo de las Nieves

A road turns off here towards the east to the striking monolith Roque Nublo and to Pozo de las Nieves. From a parking lot a few miles further on it is possible to make the short climb up ⑦ ✱ ✱ **Roque Nublo**. Then continue the trip towards the east to the summit of ⑧ ✱ ✱ **Pozo de las Nieves**, Gran Canaria's highest peak (from Ayacata 9km/5.5mi one way). On clear days there is a fantastic view of the island from the peak.

The next part of the tour, to Tejeda, also has some interesting views. The route to the mountain village of ⑨**Tejeda** has many curves, and from here Cruz de Tejeda, the highest point on the pass (1,490m/4,888ft), is another 7km/4mi away. There is almost always lots of activity around the cross. Fruit and souvenirs are sold from stands and various restaurants encourage visitors to stop.

Side trip to Pinar de Tamabada

Turn off shortly after Cruz de Tejeda towards the »cave village« of ⑩ ✱ ✱ **Artenara** amidst a wonderfully untouched landscape. There are two restaurants here with views for an enjoyable break. ⑪ ✱ **Pinar de Tamadaba** is an inviting place to hike and picnic. The distance from Cruz de Tejeda to Pinar de Tamadaba and back is 50km/30mi, to Artenara and back about 38km/22mi.

The main route runs from Cruz de Tejeda towards the east to ⑫ **Vega de San Mateo**. Turn off onto the GC 41 in the town. The route passes the Museo La Cantonera (closed) to ⑬**Valsequillo**. The fields around the town are used in part for dry farming. In January and February, when the almond trees are blossoming, the area is especially beautiful. Then it is a quick 11km/7mi from Valsequillo to ⑭ **Telde**, the island's second-largest city. The Iglesia de San Juan Bautista is well worth a visit. Those less interested in art will soon leave the bustling town behind and take the motorway back to the south.

Tour 3 Through the south on the trail of the Guanches

Start and finish: Playa del Inglés
Length: 125km/75mi

Duration: at least 5 hours

Route 3 explores several interesting archaeological sites from the time of the early inhabitants of the Canary Islands. The theme park Mundo Aborigen depicts the life of the early inhabitants. This tour also leads to many natural wonders.

ataga:
One of the most beautiful mountain villages

Santa Lucía
Tasty papas arrugadas with mojo at Hao restaurant

✶✶Barranco de Guayadeque

Santa Lucía **5** 16 km **8** Ingenio **10** Cuatro Puertas 3 km 7 km

2 km Agüimes **7** 10 km 3 km **9**

Fataga **4** 1 km **6** 20 km 40 km

4 km ✶**Fortaleza Grande**

3 Arteara

5 km

2 ✶**Mundo Aborigen**

6 km

1 ✶✶**Playa del Inglés/ Maspalomas**

Mundo Aborigen
Replica of an early Canarian village

For this route take the road that runs from **❶Playa del Inglés** northwards into the mountains. The theme park **❷ ✶ Mundo Aborigen** is only 6km/4mi away and gives an interesting picture of the life of the early islanders. The next stop is **❸Arteara**, where the Parque Arqueológico de Arteara was opened in 2004. It includes a cemetery

DON'T MISS

- A visit to the outdoor museum Mundo Aborigen
- Lunch at the rustic restaurant Hao
- A side trip to the historic Fortaleza Grande
- A drive through Barranco de Guayadeque with a break at a cave restaurant

from the time of the Guanches and a visitor centre with background information. The next part of the trip has many impressive views of the grandeur of the mountains. Drive through the palm-shaded village of ❹**Fataga** and after 8km/5mi turn off right towards ❺**Santa Lucía**. The mosque-like dome of the village church can be seen from far off. The restaurant Hao with a little museum attached is a good place to take a break. 2km/1¼mi beyond Santa Lucía a road turns right off the GC 65 towards La Sorrueda (signed Ansite). Drive through the hamlet with its pretty palm trees. The road ends about 3km/2mi after leaving the main road at a parking lot. From here it is just a short walk uphill to ❻✳ **Fortaleza Grande**. These rocks were sacred to the Guanches and the site of the last decisive battle against the Spanish conquerors. Return to the main road and drive 22km/12mi to ❼**Agüimes**, where the central square with its ancient trees is very pretty. At the northern edge of town follow the signs to ❽✳✳ **Barranco de Guayadeque**, an impressive gorge with lush vegetation. Note the caves which were used by the Guanches as homes. To spend a little time in one of these caves, try one of the two restaurants in Barranco. A little museum about 3km/2mi beyond Agüimes on the left has more background information on Guanche culture.

Follow the same road back through the barranco. After 7km/4mi (from the end of the barranco) keep left and follow a very narrow lane to ❾**Ingenio**. The craft shop here with drawn-work embroidery is more interesting than the little rock museum. The GC 100 connects Ingenio with Telde. After 7km/4mi a lane turns off to the ❿**Cuatro Puertas**; you can drive to within about 200m/200yd of the cave with its four large entrances. On the southern slope there are more caves that were inhabited by the Guanches.
Return to Playa del Inglés via the GC 140; after 4km/2.5mi it meets the Las Palmas – ❶**Playa del Inglés** motorway.

Tour 4 Highlights in the north

Start and finish: Las Palmas
Length: 120km/70mi

Duration: at least 5 hours

This tour goes to the north with its rich vegetation. There are pretty little towns and interesting sights on the way. The roads are in part winding, so the tour takes a relatively long time.

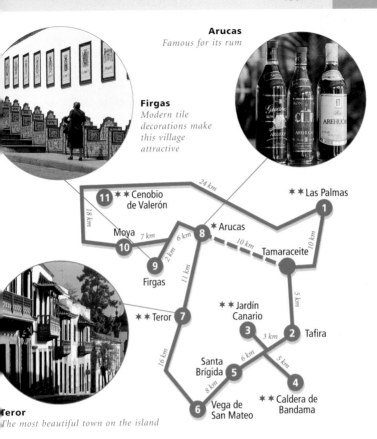

Arucas
Famous for its rum

Firgas
Modern tile decorations make this village attractive

Teror
The most beautiful town on the island

Leave **❶ ＊＊ Las Palmas** on the GC 100 towards **❷ Tafira**. The many villas set in large gardens show that this is the area where Gran Canaria's wealthy residents live. Don't miss visiting the **❸ ＊＊ Jardín Canario** below Tafira Alta. Then follow the main road, GC 100. In Monte Coello turn off left towards Pico de Bandama. The observation point on the peak offers an excellent view as far as Las Palmas and down into the **❹ ＊＊ Caldera de Bandama**. At the foot of Pico de Bandama a road runs south to Campo de Golf and on to La Atalaya, which is on almost every organized island tour. About 3km/2mi to the north of La Atalaya rejoin the GC 15. Follow it for 2km/1¼mi to **❺ Santa Brígida**, an attractive town of villas. The next town of any size is **❻ Vega de San Mateo**, which is especially busy on Sundays because of the livestock market. In Vega de San Mateo turn on-to the GC 42 towards **❼ ＊＊ Teror**, which many people consider the prettiest town on Gran Canaria. When walking around the town note the many balconies with artistic woodcarving. The next stop is **❽* Arucas** north of Teror. After touring the elaborately decorated neo-Gothic church, a drive up to Montaña de Arucas is worthwhile. Arucas' local mountain offers a good panoramic view (restaurant).

Shortening the tour

If you tire of the endless winding roads or are familiar with the north from other visits, return to Las Palmas from Arucas via Tamaraceite. The drive offers impressive views of the capital and Isleta off the coast.

The main route runs from Arucas westwards to **❾Firgas**, which is known on the eastern Canary Islands for its mineral spring. The lush and blooming vegetation in the area, a result of the plentiful water supply, is more interesting than the town. From Firgas take the same road back to Buenlugar, and from there west to **❿Moya**. It won't take long to see the town, but a side trip to Barranco de Moya with the last remains of Gran Canaria's laurel woods (Los Tilos) is worthwhile. The road then winds down to the coast. Just before meeting the GC2, a winding road branches off right to **⓫** **★ ★ Cenobio de Valerón**. The cave complex is located underneath a basalt arch and probably represents the most impressive remains of the Guanches. The road offers magnificent views of the section of coast called Cuesta de Silva. After a few miles it meets the GC2, which runs along the coast and back to **❶ ★ ★ Las Palmas**.

Tour 5 By Jeep into lonely country

Start and finish: Playa del Inglés
Length: 160km/96mi

Duration: at least 5 hours

Even though the winding road in the interior of the island is paved, except for a short section, it is in such bad condition that it is impassable in a normal vehicle. After a rainy period – especially in the winter – a Jeep might have problems, too. The road is often very busy at weekends!

From **❶Playa del Inglés** take the coast road heading west. At the fishing village of **❷Arguineguín** take the well-surfaced road north into the interior through the **❸ ★ Barranco de Arguineguín**, passing the town of Cercado Espino and then winding up to **❹ Embalse de Soria** (Soria Reservoir). Then the road becomes worse. It runs along the west and north shore of the reservoir and after a few miles meets a paved road again. At

DON'T MISS
- A short walk at Embalse de Soria
- A tour of the cave town Artenara and a meal with cave atmosphere
- The narrow road to San Nicolás de Tolentino
- Supper at the yacht harbour of Puerto de Mogán

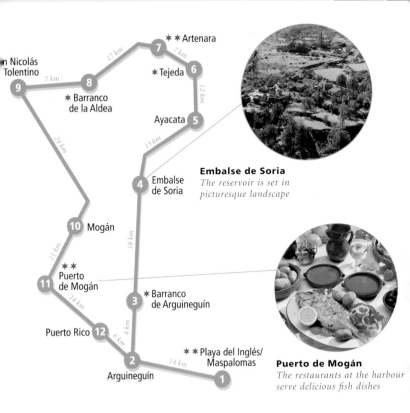

Embalse de Soria
The reservoir is set in picturesque landscape

Puerto de Mogán
The restaurants at the harbour serve delicious fish dishes

⑤ Ayacata it joins the main road through the interior. Follow this north and enjoy the many changing views of the mountains. Just beyond ⑥ ✳ **Tejeda** at Cruz de Tejeda turn off left towards ⑦ ✳✳ **Artenara**. After seeing the cave homes and the cave church try one of the two restaurants here, which have outstanding food and a magnificent view of the highest peaks of the island.

From Artenara drive 4km/2.5mi westwards and turn off left towards San Nicolás de Tolentino. Now comes the most beautiful part of the entire route. It leads through secluded mountains on an asphalted but narrow and winding road. The road through ⑧ ✳ **Barranco de la Aldea** passes several reservoirs and finally reaches ⑨ **San Nicolás de Tolentino**. To return to the starting point follow the main road from here southwards via ⑩ **Mogán**, ⑪ ✳✳ **Puerto de Mogán** and ⑫ **Puerto Rico**. This route is described as part of the trip around the island (►p.109). One of the restaurants in the yacht harbour of Puerto de Mogán makes a good place to end the day.

Sights
from A to Z

MAGNIFICENT DUNES,
GREAT BEACHES,
FRAGRANT PINE FORESTS,
BIZARRE ROCK FORMATIONS AND
PRETTY COASTAL VILLAGES LIKE
PUERTO DE MOGÁN PICTURED HERE SHOW THE
CHARM OF THE THIRD-LARGEST CANARY ISLAND.

★ Agaete

B 2

Elevation: 41m/133ft above sea level **Population:** 5,600 (entire district)

Agaete lies in north-western Gran Canaria at the foot of Mount Tamadaba and is the capital of the district of the same name. Many tourists come here on trips to the fertile Barranco de Agaete.

The residents still live mainly from agriculture. In the past agricultural products were shipped from the nearby harbour, ▶ Puerto de las Nieves.

Agaete's white houses give it a friendly appearance; it is a rural town that has not lost its authenticity. The **plaza** in front of the Iglesia de la Concepción is the focal point. Old and young gather here under shady trees. It is a good place to start a short tour of the town. Narrow lanes and alleys, and houses with pretty wooden balconies give the town its atmosphere.

What to See in Agaete

Iglesia de la Concepción The simple Iglesia de la Concepción was built in the late 19th century to replace an earlier church. Every year during the **Bajada de la Rama** (4–7 August) the church is the centre of the town's activities. The festival is held to ask Nuestra Señora de las Nieves for enough rain for the next months.

Huerto de las Flores Follow Calle Huertas, which starts at the church plaza, a short distance to the **flower garden** Huerto de las Flores. The small, somewhat overgrown garden has impressive examples of Canarian and tropical plants (hours: Mon–Fri 9am–1pm).

Around Agaete

Cueva de las Cruces Leave Agaete and drive towards Gáldar; after 5km/3mi on the right is the Cueva de las Cruces (**Cave of Crosses**). Its name is supposed to have come from the crosses that were carved into the cave walls by the Spanish conquistadors. Scientists believe that the caves were adapted to the needs of the early Canarians. Thus the hole in the roof of the cave served as a chimney. There is another theory that the caves were not used as living quarters but only made later in the process of building roads in the area.

Reptilandia To get to the reptile park, drive from Agaete and turn left shortly after the Cueva de las Cruces towards Sardina del Norte; then follow the signs to the right to Reptilandia Park. The park has more than 500 lizards, snakes, frogs, crocodiles, turtles, tarantulas and other an-

Idyllic: the lush and fertile Barranco de Agaete

imals in outdoor terrariums and a reptile house. The snake feeding on Sunday afternoon is interesting (hours: daily 11am–5.30pm). ⏰

One of the most beautiful barrancos on the island stretches southeast from Agaete. Many day-trippers come at weekends, and generally stop at one of the restaurants on the main road to the barranco. During the week the picturesque valley offers rest and seclusion. Barranco de Agaete has a lush, partially tropical vegetation due to the generous water supply and the shelter offered by the steep valley walls. Lemon, orange, mango and avocado trees flourish between palms. The farmers in this area are especially proud of their coffee plants.

★
Barranco de Agaete

From Agaete the road into Barranco de Agaete passes farms and holiday accommodation. After 8km/5mi comes the village Los Berrazales. When no tour buses stop, time seems to have stood still here. Los Berrazales was known as a **spa** in the past. The iron-rich spring water was considered to have health benefits. In the meantime it has proved more profitable to bottle the water and sell it as mineral

Los Berrazales

▶ **VISITING AGAETE**

WHERE TO EAT

▶ **Moderate**

Casa Romántica
On the main road running through Barranco de Agaete (at km 3.5)
Tel. 928 89 80 84
Garden restaurant with international cuisine. A good place for a coffee break, too. The cakes are made on the premises; the fruits are from the house garden (lunch daily 12.30pm–5pm).

WHERE TO STAY

▶ **Budget**

Hotel Princesa Guayarmina
Los Berrazales
Tel. 928 89 80 09
Fax 928 89 85 25
www.hotelguayarmina.com
This hotel is for people who want to do it on their own. You won't find it in any travel catalogue. It used to be frequented by spa guests; today hikers and nature lovers stop off here for short stays. The rooms are simply furnished, so don't expect too much comfort. During the week you might even have the sundeck and pool to yourself.

▶ **Mid-range**

Finca Las Longueras Hotel Rural
Agaete
Tel. 928 89 81 45
Fax 928 89 87 52
www.laslongueras.com
The »red house« was built in 1895 in the middle of an extensive plantation. It has 1 suite and 9 double rooms, as well as a separate house. Cosy court-yards and a swimming pool are inviting places to relax.

water. Little is left to remind visitors of the former spa; some of the houses stand empty.

Stroll ▶ The paved road, which is hardly ever used, ends just below the **Princesa Guayarmina** hotel. A path leads uphill from here and the valley ends after about 1.5km/1mi. The houses of El Sao can be seen above the steep valley walls.

Agüimes

C 4

Elevation: 286m/943ft above sea level   **Population:** 14,000 (entire district)

Agüimes, about halfway between Las Palmas and Maspalomas, is generally only a stop on the way to Barranco de Guayadeque.

The locals derive their income mainly from agriculture, concentrating on tomatoes. Cacti are also grown in large numbers here. The plants flourish here in alkali-poor soil and excellent climatic conditions. It takes about three years until the cacti are large enough to export.

Agüimes has an attractive town centre. Many of the pretty old cottages around the church and the shady plaza are being restored. Construction of the **Iglesia de San Sebastián** began in the 18th century, but was only completed in the mid-19th century. Its large dome is reminiscent of oriental structures. Some of the statues of saints inside are attributed to Luján Pérez.

Around Agüimes

Do not expect too much if you plan to visit Parque de Cocodrilos: various kinds of deer, dwarf donkeys, ponies, ostriches, baboons, crocodiles and other animals live here, but much too close together. There is also a crocodile and parrot show several times a day. To get to the zoo drive from Cruce de Arinaga (6km/3.5mi south-east of Agüimes) towards Los Corralillos; the zoo is on the right-hand side of the road. Buses also run from some of the hotels in the south to the zoo (hours: Mon– Fri, Sun 10am–5pm).

Parque de Cocodrilos

Twilight in the streets of Agüimes

▶ VISITING AGÜIMES

WHERE TO EAT

▶ Moderate
La Farola
Calle Alcalá Gallano
On the Arinaga jetty
Tel. 928 18 02 24
This well-known seafood restaurant specializes in lobsters that it raises itself. The seating is right along the jetty in a nautical atmosphere; it pays to make reservations on the weekend.

▶ Inexpensive
Tagoror
At the end of Barranco de Guayadeque
Tel. 928 17 20 13
Cave restaurant with a terrace and a good selection of tapas. The rest of the menu is more international than Canarian.

WHERE TO STAY

▶ Budget
Hotel Rural Casa de los Camellos
Calle Progreso 12
Tel. 928 78 50 03
Fax 928 78 50 53
www.hecansa.com
A former camel station near the church with twelve comfortable and individually furnished rooms. The little country hotel with a large courtyard is run by a school for hotel management.

Arinaga

From Cruce de Arinaga drive 5km/3mi east to the **fishing village** of Arinaga. The town itself is not very attractive with its apartment buildings. The new promenade along the sea does not change this impression. Arinaga has one of the few remaining desalination works on Gran Canaria. **Playa de Arinaga** is sheltered in a broad bay and attracts mainly the locals; surfers consider it to be a good shallow surfing area.

★ ★
Barranco de Guayadeque

North of Agüimes, Barranco de Guayadeque is a nature reserve because of the many endemic plants that grow here. The valley is especially beautiful in spring, when everything seems to be blooming everywhere. Grain and vegetables are grown without modern technology on small fields full of poppies.

The farmers transport their hay on donkeys. If it weren't for the tour buses and tourists in hire cars, the place would look as if time had stood still one hundred years ago.

Barranco de Guayadeque has one other unique characteristic: in the steep walls of the valley there are many **caves**. Some of these caves are natural, and some are man-made; they were used as living quarters and burial sites by the pre-Hispanic inhabitants. Some of the caves are still occupied; others are difficult to reach due to landslides. This is probably why so many artefacts, including pottery, clothing, bones and mummies, were found here. Some of them are in the **museum** that is situated 3km/2mi north of Agüimes on the drive to the barranco.

Follow the paved road further into the barranco to see more cave dwellings after about 2km/1¼mi. The cave restaurant and cave church are also worth visiting. A narrow path leads up to inhabited caves; others are used as stables or storerooms. Luxuriant floral decoration completes the idyllic scene. After 5km/3mi the road ends at another **cave restaurant**, where the outside tables have a beautiful view over the valley.

Continue on foot from here on a path past some more cave huts for magnificent views of the unusual mountains.

◄ Stroll

Lomo de los Letreros is a mountain range near **Barranco de Balos**, only a few miles west of Agüimes. The name »Los Letreros« (»the inscriptions«) reveals why visitors and souvenir hunters have been coming to the 300m/1,000ft-long cliff for years. Simple but sometimes quite bizarre human figures were carved into the rock and later discovered here.

Lomo de los Letreros

The figure of a boat with a curved prow has attracted a lot of attention, as it is the first sign that the early Canarians had boats. Simple geometric patterns, spirals and circles have also been found here. Visitors will not see much of this today without an experienced guide since the carvings are worn away by wind and weather, and many tourists felt that they had to leave their own marks behind. The area is fenced off.

However, if you want to try your luck, leave Agüimes on the GC 550 towards Santa Lucía; after about 3km/2mi a road turns off to the left towards the hamlet Los Corralillos (it curves back to Cruce de Arinaga). 1km/0.5mi after Los Corralillos follow the path on the right on foot down into Barranco de Balos.

 Baedeker TIP

Rural holidays

»Turismo rural«, »rural tourism«, is no insider tip anymore on the Canary Islands. Agüimes played a pioneering role in the venture and now has accommodation for about 50 guests in two small hotels and several country homes. The Grantural website (www.ecoturismocanarias.com, tel. 928 39 01 69, 35003 Las Palmas, Calle Perojo 36) has information on them and other attractive holiday stays.

Arguineguín

D 2

Elevation: Sea level   **Population:** 4,500

The days as a quiet fishing village are long gone. Only 12km/7mi west of the tourist centre of Maspalomas, Arguineguín has developed into a popular tourist centre itself with a Canarian touch.

Coming from Maspalomas, Arguineguín does not look very attractive at first with the cement factory dominating the scene, but the picturesque **fishing port** is different. Excursion boats depart from here, and there are regular connections to Puerto Rico and Puerto de Mogán. Restaurants in every class from simple to luxurious line the port road. Many of them have a wonderful view of the harbour and the sea. While holiday-makers – including many long-term guests – have to make do with tiny beaches and a not very attractive setting, they appreciate the fact that the place was not planned on a drawing board.

From Arguineguín the road to Soría reservoir in the mountainous interior is winding and narrow

▶ VISITING ARGUINEGUÍN

SHOPPING

Mercado
Around the harbour
Tue 8am–2pm
The selection is huge: fruit, vegetables, fish and meat, but also crafts, clothing and much more.

WHERE TO EAT

▶ Inexpensive
Casa Fernando
Embalse de Soria
(below the city wall)
Tel. 928 17 23 46
Day-trippers meet in the bar for typical Canarian cooking; hours: daily 10am–6pm.

▶ Moderate
Cofradía de Pescadores
At the harbour
Tel. 928 15 09 63
The fish lands on the table right from the boat; open from noon straight through (closed Mon and Tue).

▶ Expensive
Puerto Atlántico
On the road to Mogán (km 68(mi 41)
Tel. 928 15 06 36
Luxury restaurant with creative in-ternational food. There is an excellent selection of Spanish wine. Good service is a matter of course here.

WHERE TO STAY

▶ Mid-range
Apartments Aquamarina
Carretera General del Sur
Patalavaca
Tel. 928 73 51 25
Fax 928 15 20 97
Choose between a tastefully furnished apartment or a bungalow. The greenery makes for attractive sur-roundings.

▶ Luxury
La Canaria
Carretera General del Sur
(km 69/mi 42)
Patalavaca
Tel. 928 15 04 00, fax 928 15 10 03
www.hoteles.dunas.com
Only the best is good enough here. The quiet, large rooms all have a view of the sea and lushly planted balco-nies. There is a pool area of 2,000 sq m/21,400 sq ft with seawater and freshwater pools. The kitchen has an excellent reputation and four restau-rants provide variety.

Around Arguineguín

Arguineguín and Patalavaca are connected by a promenade. The main road does not hint at the exclusive hotels that line the coast here – especially the La Canaria. Here you can eat in a restaurant away from the usual tourist crowd or cross the bridge to offshore La Isleta with its pretty parks. The white sand on **Playa de la Verga** to the west was imported from the Caribbean.

Patalavaca

Driving to Barranco de Arguineguín and on to the centre of the is-land is a popular weekend pastime for Canarians. Many Jeep safaris

✶
Barranco de
Arguineguín

offer this tour as well. Almost all of the route is paved now but the short section between the Soria Reservoir and Cruz de San Antonio is so bad that it is usually impassable for normal cars. Even with a Jeep it can take a long time. The 50km/30mi from Arguineguín to Ayacata (including a side trip to Embalse de Soria) takes at least two hours without longer stops.

From Arguineguín drive east on the paved road into the barranco. The lower part of the valley is dry and no one lives there. But the higher the elevation, the more settlements appear until they actually merge with each other. The area is agricultural, producing citrus fruits, papaya and wine.

▶ Embalse de Soria

After the hamlet of **Cercado Espino** the road gets narrower and the barranco ends soon afterwards. The road then winds up the mountain. Just 8km/5mi after Cercado de Espino the road divides, the right branch leading to the picturesque Soria Reservoir after 2km/1¼mi. The dam Embalse de Soria was completed in 1971, but the reservoir has never been completely full. The area offers excellent hiking; a trail follows the northern edge of the reservoir. For **Embalse de Cueva de las Niñas** go back to the fork in the road, turn right and continue northwards. Since the road is not very good the next ten kilometres (six miles) will be slow going. The beautiful view of the reservoir surrounded by pine forests compensates for the drive. There are picnic areas for those who want to rest awhile. The road gets better again after this and soon is paved again. The drive on to **Ayacata** becomes quite enjoyable.

★ ★ Artenara

B 3

Elevation: 1,251m/4,104ft above sea level

Population: 1,600 (entire district)

The landscape around the mountain village of Artenara in north-western Gran Canaria is still relatively untouched. Artenara is the highest settlement on the island. Tourists come here to visit the cave church and to get an impression of the local culture.

At first glance Artenara seems no different from any other Canarian mountain village. But a closer look reveals that many of the residents still live in caves. These »caves« have been given normal house façades. Life in the village is not primitive: TV antennae are visible on many of the houses and the kitchens have modern appliances.

What to See in Artenara

Iglesia de la Virgen de la Cuevita

To reach the **cave church**, Iglesia de la Virgen de la Cuevita, follow the street opposite the church in the centre of town (near the Casa

▶ VISITING ARTENARA

INFORMATION

Oficina de Turismo
Camino La Silla
Tel. 928 66 61 02
With a small art gallery.

SHOPPING

Centro de Recuperación de Artesanía
At the bus parking lot
The items sold here were really braided, woven or created by local craftsmen (closed Mon).

WHERE TO EAT

▶ Moderate

La Esquina
Town centre, near the church
Tel. 928 66 63 81
The terrace offers a sensational view of the mountains. Canarian food. Open daily except Mon.

WHERE TO STAY

▶ Budget

El Pajar
Reservations with Grantural
Tel. 928 39 01 69
www.ecoturismocanarias.com
The spacious cave dwelling has a living room, three bedrooms, kitchen and a terrace with a small garden. Situated right on the mountainside, it has a wonderful view of the Caldera of Tejeda.

Rustic cave restaurant in Artenara

Baedeker TIP

Exploded

GC 110 between Artenara and Valleseco has an astonishing view of the island's most recent volcano. Caldera Pinos del Gáldar was probably formed about 3,000 years ago by a massive explosion that blew the top of the volcano away and left the impressive crater. The observation point lies 1,510m/4,954ft above sea level and has a wonderful view of the north coast. On a clear day you might even see Pico de Teide on Tenerife.

Consistorial) uphill. It ends just a few feet in front of the cave church, which can be recognized by the bell above the entrance. The church is dedicated to the Virgin of the Cave, the patron saint of cyclists and folk musicians. No one knows the exact age of the church, but it was probably only carved out of the rock a few decades ago.

Around Artenara

Pinar de Tamadaba

Tamadaba Forest lies at an elevation of 1,400m/4,600ft and can only be reached by car from Artenara (about 8km/5mi). The most beautiful, but somewhat sparse, pine forest on Gran Canaria is a fitting reward for the drive on a winding road. Spanish moss hangs from many of the tall, slender trees. The **mirador** at the end of the road that leads into the Pinar de Tamadaba has a wonderful view of the coast.

In late August the »Feast of the Virgin of the Cave« is celebrated with enthusiasm

4km/2.5mi after Artenara on the road that connects it to Pinar de Tamadaba, a trail turns off to the south. It is relatively easy to drive up to **Acusa**, then the road winds steeply down the mountain. While the drive is not always easy in a normal car, the beautiful and isolated mountain landscape is an ample reward. After a while the road passes the Embalse de Parralillo and then other reservoirs. After about two hours the houses of ►**San Nicolás de Tolentino** appear.

✳ Arucas

B 3

Elevation: 250m/825ft above sea level   **Population:** 32,500
(entire district)

Arucas lies 17km/11mi west of Las Palmas. It is the third-largest town on Gran Canaria after the capital and Telde. The pretty old part of town is dominated by the large neo-Gothic parish church. Arucas is also the home of the only rum distillery on Gran Canaria. It is open for tours.

▶ VISITING ARUCAS

INFORMATION
Oficina de Turismo
Plaza de la Constitución 2
Tel. 928 62 31 36

SHOPPING
Mercado
Saturday is market day in Arucas; the market takes place on Plaza de la Constitución and the surrounding streets.

WHERE TO EAT
▶ Moderate
Mesón de la Montaña
Montaña de Arucas
Tel. 928 60 14 75
The drive up to the volcano crater is worthwhile for the view alone. Local people enjoy this restaurant as well. The cooking is Canarian and international.

WHERE TO STAY

> *Baedeker recommendation*

> #### ▶ Moderate
> *Hacienda del Buen Suceso*
> On the Arucas –
> Bañaderos (1km/0.5mi) road
> Tel. 928 62 29 45
> Fax 928 62 29 42
> www.hotelhacienda.sitio.net
> The hacienda's history goes back to 1572. The present owners have restored it with great care and turned it into a pretty finca in the midst of banana plantations. It has 18 individually designed rooms. The restaurant has great atmosphere and is open to the general public as well.

Agriculture thrives here, as the town is located in one of the most plentifully watered parts of the island. After the Spanish conquest sugar cane was planted, but was no longer profitable after the 17th century. In the early 20th century agriculture concentrated on bananas. While the area prospered for some decades with this monoculture, it suffered when Canarian bananas became increasingly difficult to market. Large areas of the banana plantations were abandoned in the early 1980s, and the fields were converted to fruit, vegetable and flower farms.

The Arucas area was settled before the Spanish came; the early Canarians called the settlement »Arehucas«. On the nearby Montaña de Arucas a decisive battle between the leader of the early Canarians, **Doramas**, and the leader of the Spanish, Pedro de Vera, took place in 1481. Only after Doramas was wounded in an ambush was Pedro de Vera able to kill him. The Spanish officially founded Arucas in 1505.

History

What to See in Arucas

There is a modern monument to the early Canarian leader Doramas on Plaza de la Constitución, main square of Arucas.

Plaza de la Constitución

The park borders the plaza on the west. It is a fine botanical garden and once belonged to the Gourié family. Their former residence is now the **Museo Municipal** with works by Canarian artists (hours: Mon–Fri 10am–1pm and 5pm–7pm, Sat 10am–1pm).

Parque de Gourié ⏲

Follow Calle León y Castillo and Calle Gourié, where there is a magnificent dragon tree in the inner courtyard of the library, to the massive Iglesia de San Juan Bautista. Because of its size and neo-Gothic style the church, which is dedicated to John the Baptist, is often called a **cathedral**. Construction began in 1909 and the first mass was celebrated in 1917, but the last of the four towers was not completed until the 1970s. Local grey basalt was the main building material. It is especially resistant to weathering but is not easy to work. This makes the rose window above the main entrance all the more impressive. Note the colourful stained glass windows inside, and the reclining figure of Christ which was made by the sculptor Manuel Ramos (1899–1971), a native of Arucas.

Iglesia de San Juan Bautista

About 500m/1,650ft west of the town centre along the road going to Guía is the Garden of the Hesperides (Jardín de las Hespérides). Among the aged trees there are varieties of palms and a large dragon tree. This garden is surrounded by giant banana plantations. It be-

Jardín de Hespérides

← *It looks much older, but the cathedral of Arucas was only completed in the 1970s*

Rum from Arucas

longs to the Massieu family and is open to the public every day except Sunday.

The production of **rum** has a long history in Arucas. Destilería Arehucas (on the edge of town going towards Guía) started out in 1884 as a sugar factory. Today it employs about 50 people, who produce about 3 million litres of rum of various kinds every year.

»Ron Añejo«, a twelve-year-old rum is considered to be exceptional. The distillery also produces a variety of »specialties«, like rum with honey (Ron Miel) or rum with milk and lemon (Leche Rizada). Tours of the factory are available (hours: Mon–Fri 10am–1pm or 2pm in the winter). The tour includes a display of oak barrels with the autographs of prominent guests. They include Plácido Domingo and Juan Carlos I. There is also a tasting room where the different varieties of rum can be sampled.

✳ **Destilería Arehucas**

Around Arucas

✳ **Montaña de Arucas**

Just north of the town centre stands Montaña de Arucas (412m/1,352ft above sea level). A narrow road starts at the church (signposted) and ends on a large parking lot with a restaurant. There is a wonderful **panoramic view** from the top.

✳ ✳ Caldera de Bandama · Pico de Bandama

B 4

About 10km/6mi south of Las Palmas Caldera de Bandama is a reminder of the island's volcanic legacy. The almost perfectly round crater is the result of a massive eruption that took place 5,000 years ago. From the nearby Pico de Bandama (569m/1,867ft) there is a wonderful view of the crater and the rooftops of the capital city.

Drive to the caldera via Monte Lentiscal, where a side road branches off the GC 15 and leads to the observation area (with cafeteria) on the peak of Pico de Bandama. On the way to the top there are beautiful views of Caldera de Bandama. The crater is about 1,000m/3,300ft across and 200m/660ft deep. There is an abandoned farm on its floor. Some of the surrounding fields are still in use, but it takes a lot of effort to farm here since only a small path leads into the crater.

In order to preserve the natural setting, a special permit is necessary to climb down into the crater. This can be obtained at the Cabildo Insular in Las Palmas. A permit is not necessary to **hike around the crater**, which takes about an hour, but the hike is only for people who are sure of foot and unafraid of heights. From Bandama follow the road to Pico de Bandama. After about 10 minutes, in a left-hand curve, leave the road and follow a broad trail to the edge of the caldera. From here a path goes around the edge of the crater. The last part of the hike passes through the property of the Bandama golf hotel. The **golf course** was established in the late 19th century by an Englishman and is the oldest in Spain. Follow the hotel driveway to the main road leading to Pico de Bandama and the starting point of the hike.

CALDERA DE BANDAMA

WHERE TO EAT

► **Mid-range**
Hotel Golf Bandama
Carretera Bandama
Tel. 928 35 15 38
Fax 928 35 01 10
www.bandamagolf.com
The little family-run hotel is right next to the golf course. For those who want a change from golf there is a swimming pool, tennis court and riding stable (lessons upon request).

✶ ✶ Cenobio de Valerón

B 3

Cenobio de Valerón is one of the most significant archaeological sites on the Canary Islands. The cave complex has posed many riddles to archaeologists. Until well into the 20th century it was presumed to be a religious site for the early Canarians that was shrouded in myth.

Coming from Guía follow the winding coastal road marked »Cuesta de Silva« eastwards to Cenobio de Valerón. After a thorough restoration the caves have been open to the public again since 2007. The lighting for photography is best in the morning.

⏲
Opening hours:
Tue–Sun 10am–5pr

Cenobio de Valerón is a complex of 298 caves under a natural basalt arch that is about 30m/100ft wide and 25m/80ft high. In the soft tuff stone, which is easy to work even with simple tools, the early Canarians created caves on various levels and adapted natural caves. They

Cave palace

Steeped in mystery to this day – the Cenobio de Valerón

were separated by wooden doors and connected by corridors and stairs. The complex eventually became a real cave palace. In one of the caves higher up simple geometric patterns are carved into the wall.

Monastery or grain store? ►

There has been much speculation in the past as to the purpose of these caves. Earlier historians called Cenobio de Valerón the **cave monastery of the harimaguadas**, holy virgins who lived here as priestesses. Another version has it that young women spent some time here before they got married. A rich diet was supposed to help them gain weight to ensure that they would have many offspring. Latest research has departed from these mythological explanations. It is possible that the cave palace was simply used to **store grain**.

Old sources have revealed that Cenobio de Valerón used to be decorated much more richly than it is today. Pedro Agustín del Castillo y Ruiz Vergara described it as follows: »When I had occasion to go to the Guía area, two of the town leaders asked if I would like to see one of the monasteries of these ancient people, which was located at a high and steep place above Barranco de Valerón. They guided me there at considerable risk. I admit that I was amazed at the structure. There was a large arch carved into a cliff – without sharp iron instruments, which the ancient people did not have, but only with flint splinters mounted on wooden handles that were used like axes and picks to work wood and cut down trees. Under the arch a corridor led inside and there was a large number of cells or rooms on both sides: one above the other and all with windows. On each side of the entrance there was a kind of tower, which was accessible from inside and had windows facing the depths of the barranco.«

On the peak above Cenobio de Valerón there was a tagoror, a place   **Tagoror**
of assembly. The stone seats can still be seen.
The summit commands a wonderful view of the section of coast called **Cuesta de Silva**. It was named after Diego de Silva, who tried to land on Gran Canaria's north coast during the Spanish conquest.

Cruz de Tejeda

B 3

Cruz de Tejeda marks the highest point on the pass in the centre of Gran Canaria (1,490m/4,888ft). Almost all tour buses stop at the stone cross.

This is a commercial and chaotic place. Fruit and sweets are on sale in stands, and before you can turn around you will have been photographed with a donkey – for a fee of course. Cruz de Tejeda is known for its grand mountain panorama. The Spanish poet and philosopher Miguel de Unamuno (► Famous People) called the landscape a »petrified storm«.

 VISITING CRUZ DE TEJEDA

WHERE TO EAT

► Moderate
Asador de Yolanda
Tel. 928 66 62 76
The restaurant at Cruz de Tejeda is busy when the weather is good. It serves hearty grilled food such as lamb shanks with papas arrugadas and steamed vegetables, accompanied by local wines. The balcony on the first floor is a nice place to eat.

WHERE TO SLEEP

► Mid-range
El Refugio
Tel. 928 66 65 13
Fax 928 66 65 20
www.hotelruralelrefugio.com
The ten rooms in this country hotel with a pool will satisfy even the most demanding guests. The restaurant serves good Canarian cuisine.

Only a few steps from the pass stands the **Parador** (closed), which was designed by Néstor de la Torre and his brother Miguel (▶ Famous People) in the typical Canarian style.

North-west of Cruz de Tejeda there is a **hiking trail** with beautiful views to the residential caves of Caballero (round trip about 2 hours 30 minutes). From Cruz de Tejeda take the GC 150 towards Gáldar. After 150m/500ft comes a parking lot. From there take the left-hand trail (signed Parque Rural El Nublo) to the water reservoir. After a steep start the panoramic route meets the GC 150 again after about a half hour. Follow it to the left to **Mirador de las Palomas** and continue on the paved path. After 15 minutes follow the intersecting trail to the left to **Cruz de los Morriscos**. It takes about ten minutes from the crossing to Cuevas del Caballero. The entrances to the caves are closed off but the magnificent panorama including the Roque Nublo and Roque Bentaiga rising up out of Caldera de Tejeda is well worth the hike.

Hike to Cuevas del Caballero

Fataga

Elevation: 680m/2,231ft above sea level   **Population:** 1,000

Fataga is a pretty, typically Canarian mountain village in the barranco of the same name. It is worth stopping here on a trip from the tourist centres in southern Gran Canaria to the central mountains.

There is enough water in and around Fataga to farm small fields. Almond and apricot trees flourish here. One of the area's specialties is »tarta de almendras«, a sweet and rich but delicious almond cake. The apricot harvest in early May begins with a festival every year. The high points are a bicycle race and fireworks at midnight.
There are no special sights in Fataga, but the atmosphere is worth taking in. It is best to leave the car on the main road near the late 19th-century church and take one of the narrow streets into the centre. There are pretty white houses with lush floral decorations to delight the eye. A few bars or restaurants offer refreshments and meals.

Around Fataga

The route from Fataga and the village of Arteara 5km/3mi to the south leads through pretty countryside. Palms sway in the wind between fields. Arteara is the starting point for camel safaris (on the right-hand side of the main road when coming from Fataga). Ano-

Arteara

▶ VISITING FATAGA

WHERE TO EAT

▶ **Inexpensive**
El Albaricoque
Tel. 928 79 86 56
Snacks and tapas are on the menu. The terrace has seating with a wonderful view. There are also two simple rooms to rent.

WHERE TO STAY

▶ **Mid-range**
Finca Molino del Agua
Tel. 928 17 20 89
Fax 928 17 22 44
This pretty country hotel with 20 individually furnished rooms is 1km/ 0.5mi north of Fataga. Molino del Agua is also a good place to eat. The terrace restaurant has mainly grilled dishes.

ther attraction is the **Parque Arqueológico de Arteara** with a small visitor centre and paths leading through an ancient Canarian cemetery. The more than 800 burial sites, many of which are now only recognizable to experts, were made between 500 BC and *c* AD 1700. Signs describe the burial rites and construction of the graves. (Hours: Mon–Fri 10.30am–2.30pm).

Hike to Arteara It is possible to hike from Fataga to Arteara. There is a path parallel to the road. At first it runs east of the main road; later it switches to the west side. Leave the main road at the southern edge of Fataga and turn off to the right (coming from Maspalomas) onto the paved way that is marked »Los Llanos«. It leads past the cemetery and then zigzags down the hill. When the path branches keep left, and after about one hour you will pass a farm. Follow it to the right and soon you will be back on the Maspalomas – Fataga road. Follow the road for a short distance and turn off to the right on a path marked »Presa de Ayagaures«. It passes the **Arteara reservoir** and leads to the bottom of Fataga canyon. Soon the aforementioned camel safari station appears. Unfortunately the path ends in the brush soon afterwards.

Firgas

B 3

Elevation: 500m/1,650ft above sea level   **Population:** 6,900 (entire district)

Firgas is located about 25km/15mi west of Las Palmas in fertile green countryside. There was already a settlement here in the 16th century. The name Firgas is known to everyone on the Canaries, as mineral water is bottled here.

Firgas consists of simple white houses that cover the hillsides. The **Paseo de Gran Canaria** is an attraction. The street with water cascades in the middle is bordered by seats clad with colourful ceramic tiles. Above them are the coats of arms of the 21 administrative districts of Gran Canaria. On Paseo de Canarias, the continuation of the cascade, are depictions of various Canarian landscape scenes.

In the town centre a street branches off to the Aguas de Firgas (approx. 5km/3mi). It ends above the mineral water plant, where more than 200,000 bottles are filled every day.

Aguas de Firgas

Modern decorative tiles at Paseo de Gran Canaria in Firgas

★ ★ Gáldar

B 2/3

Elevation: 143m/469ft above sea level   **Population:** 22,000 (entire district)

Gáldar, located in north-western Gran Canaria, is easy to reach on the coastal road from Las Palmas (28km/17mi). Since tourists generally only stop off in Gáldar on a tour of the island, the town has maintained much of its original atmosphere. Remains from pre-Hispanic times are a special attraction here.

At the foot of **Pico de Gáldar** (434m/1,424ft above sea level), the town is gradually merging with ▶ Santa María de Guía. No matter from which direction you approach Gáldar, the mainstay of the local economy is evident: bananas wherever you look. However, the collapse of the market for Canarian bananas has left its mark in Gáldar as well. Many of the plantations have closed in the last years. Exotic fruits or flowers are grown on some of the fields while others are fallow. Unemployment is high in Gáldar.

▶ VISITING GÁLDAR

INFORMATION

Oficina de Turismo
Edificio Heredad de Aguas
Tel. 928 89 58 55

SHOPPING

Mercado
Calle Capitán Queseda
Good and large selection of fresh regional products, including the tasty »queso de flor« from the neighbouring town of Santa María de Guía (Mon–Sat 8am–2pm).

Mercado de Artesania
Plaza de Santiago
The crafts market takes place on the first Sunday of the month on the main plaza (only mornings).

WHERE TO EAT

▶ **Moderate**
Marisquería La Fragata
Playa de Sardina
Tel. 928 88 32 96

The well-known seafood restaurant has a French owner. The daily selection swims in a large tank right at the entrance. The restaurant's name is also its theme: the interior decorations are from an old frigate (closed Mon).

WHERE TO SLEEP

▶ **Budget**
Hacienda de Anzo
Vega de Anzo
Tel. 928 55 15 55
Fax 928 55 12 44
www.haciendadeanzo.com
This little country hotel, once the house of a banana finca, has a panoramic location above the valley of Gáldar. It has an expansive garden and a pool. Some rooms are furnished exquisitely but not all have a balcony. Good value for money.

Bust of the last Guanche king in the courtyard of the Gáldar town hall

The area around Gáldar was settled before the Spanish conquest. It was the seat of one of the island's two kings. The early Canarian settlement Agaldar was located around Cueva Pintada (see p.157) with more than 60 houses and artificially constructed caves. Agaldar was inhabited from the 6th to the 16th century.

When Juan Rejón tried to conquer the island in 1478 for the Spanish crown, **Tenesor Semidan** ruled the north-western half of Gran Canaria from Gáldar. After the Spanish found him and some of his people hiding in a cave he surrendered. His forced baptism was effective: in later conflicts between the Canarians and the Spanish, Tenesor Semidan tried repeatedly to get his people to surrender and accept Christianity. Was this what earned the last guanarteme of Gáldar a monument? It was donated by the King Juan Carlos I on 24 July 1986 and stands only a few hundred metres east of the plaza in Gáldar.

What to See in Gáldar

Plaza de Santiago

Plaza de Santiago is the centre of town. It is a nice place to relax on benches under shady trees. A kiosk sells refreshments and there are many smaller shops and services in the neighbouring streets.

Iglesia de Santiago de los Caballeros

Iglesia de Santiago de los Caballeros is located on Plaza de Santiago. Construction began in 1778 and the first service was held in 1826, but the church was not completely finished until 1872, almost 100 years after it was begun.

The green **baptismal font**, which is now in the Museo de Arte Sacra (entrance on Calle Fernando Guanarteme), is supposed to have been brought to Gran Canaria from Andalusia in the late 15th century, and was thus probably used for forcible baptism of the native Canarians. In the church there are some interesting statues of saints (including *Incarnation of Christ* and *Virgin of the Rosary*), which have been attributed to Luján Pérez.

Replica of the Cueva Pintada in the Museo Canario in Las Palmas

The ayuntamiento (town hall) is only a few yards from the church on the shady plaza. When the offices are open (only mornings) it is possible to go into the courtyard and see the magnificent dragon tree (**drago**). It was planted in 1719; today there is hardly any room for its roots and branches in the courtyard.

Ayuntamiento

The little museum in Calle Drago (north of Plaza de Santiago) is dedicated to a native of Gáldar, the painter **Antonio Padrón** (1920–68). Graphics, pictures and wood and stone sculptures by the artist, who was influenced by Expressionism and Cubism, are on display in his former home and studio. The rural culture of the farmers and fishermen was the central theme of Padrón's work (hours: Mon–Fri 9am–2pm).

Casa Museo Antonio Padrón

Cueva Pintada (»painted cave«), one of the early Canarians' major legacies, has been open to the public again since mid-2006. Cueva Pintada is now part of an archaeological park with a museum, excavation sites and reconstructed early Canarian houses (hours: Tue–Sat 9.30am–6pm, Sun 11am–2pm).

✶ ✶ Parque Arqueológico Cueva Pintada

Cueva Pintada was discovered in 1873 but not restored until 1970–74. This valuable cultural treasure was closed to the public for years to prevent it from being completely destroyed, but exact replicas could be viewed in Museo Canario in ► Las Palmas. Because of its **cave paintings**, which are unique to Gran Canaria, Cueva Pintada has a special status among all the known caves. It measures about 5 x 4.5m (16 x 14ft) and is 3m/10ft high. The walls are decorated with colourful geometric patterns, including squares, triangles and concentric circles. Cueva Pintada's original function, whether as a burial site, residence or religious site, is unknown. The guided tours of the archaeological park begin with a visit to the museum, which displays many finds from early Canarian times. Two films bring the world of the early Canarians to life. The tour of the excavation site with early Canarian remains follows. A visit to Cueva Pintada and reconstructed early Canarian buildings and a farm complete the tour.

Around Gáldar

Just beyond the south-west edge of Gáldar a street branches off towards Sardina (6km/3.5mi from Gáldar). The little fishing village is a popular place for Canarian families to swim in one of the little sandy bays and eat in one of the good **fish restaurants**. At weekends the coastal road is clogged, but during the week the picturesque scenery can be enjoyed in peace. Anyone who wants to stay longer can stop off in one of the apartment buildings with an ocean view. There are almost always vacancies, except during the summer holidays.

✶ Sardina

3km/2mi away the Faro de Sardina offers an enchanting view of the coast. There is a holiday resort beyond the lighthouse.

Faro de Sardina

Drawn-work embroidery is a form of art that you can learn in Ingenio

✳ **La Guancha** One of the major archaeological excavations on the Canary Islands is located about 2km/1¼mi north of Gáldar, on the coast near **El Agujero**. The hamlet consists of one row of houses along the coast, but there is plenty of activity at weekends. Local people enjoy the stony beaches. To the left and right of the main road between the houses there are a few remains of early Canarian houses, which were excavated in 1934 and show that the inhabitants lived in round or oval houses with an area of about 30–50 sq m (300–550 sq ft).

Follow the road that runs parallel to the coast about 400m/1,300ft to the fenced, somewhat elevated burial site of La Guancha. Normally the gate is not locked and the grounds with several burial sites can be viewed at any time. The necropolises are round structures built of mortarless stone. Presumably the largest tumulus (at the highest point in the burial site) is the tomb of the nobility or ruling class. Here numerous smaller squares are grouped around two central stone chambers – possibly the burial place of the guanarteme. The chambers were once covered with stone slabs. When the necropolis was excavated in 1935, 30 mummies from the late 11th century AD were found.

Ingenio

Elevation: 339m/1,112ft above sea level   **Population:** 26,000 (entire district)

Ingenio is located just 30km/20mi south of Las Palmas, near Aeropuerto de Gando. Its name (»sugar maker«) tells us how the people supported themselves in the past. Today Ingenio is known for embroidery.

The town flourished in the 16th and 17th centuries from the production of sugar and later also rum. Today tomatoes are raised instead of sugar cane.

Ingenio is a typical Canarian village with its plain white houses and parish church. A model of a sugar cane press commemorates the past. It was set up in 1991 at the eastern edge of town on the road to Carrizal.

What to See in Ingenio

The Museum of Rocks and Canarian Crafts is at the northern edge of town. Old agricultural implements are displayed outside. The »museum« is primarily a shop for Canarian crafts. A **school for embroidery** is attached (open to the public). The rock collection has little to offer the uninitiated. Many of the exhibits are inadequately labelled or not at all. The Museo de Piedras y Artesanía Canaria is open daily 9am–6pm (free admission).

Museo de Piedras y Artesanía

! **Baedeker** TIP

Christmas spirit on Gran Canaria?
You won't see many Christmas trees, but there are beautiful nativity scenes. One of the largest and most elaborate is in the Museo de Piedras in Ingenio. The Christmas story is displayed in miniature with much love for detail, from the stable in Bethlehem to the Magi. It can be seen every year from mid-December to 6 January.

★ ★ Las Palmas

B 4

Elevation: 0m – 210m/0 – 690ft above sea level

Population: 380,000

Las Palmas de Gran Canaria is the uncontested metropolis of the Canary Isles. The capital of the eponymous province is bursting with urban life, which however includes permanent traffic jams and mass tourism on the outskirts. But the renovated old quarter, quality museums and the pulsing entertainment district of Santa Catalina make a visit to the island capital an absolute must.

Las Palmas is located on the northern point of the island. The city stretches along the coast from north to south for about 14km/8mi. The foothills of the central mountains form the border to the inner part of the island. The peninsula **La Isleta** (»the islet«) has been part of the city since the 20th century. La Isleta was once really an island, but a neck of land developed into a land bridge to Gran Canaria.

Port with international flair

With its official total of 380,000 residents (the real number is probably much higher) Las Palmas is by far the largest city on the Canaries and the seventh-largest city in Spain. It has always been a major economic, traffic and trade centre and owes its economic status to the **port** (Puerto de la Luz). Its strategic position at the intersection of shipping routes between Europe, Africa and South America turned it into one of the largest ports on the Atlantic. The city is es-

pecially proud of the **university**, which was founded in 1990. The residents of Gran Canaria fought for it for many years. Until 1990 anyone who wanted to go to university had to go to Tenerife or the Spanish mainland.

Thousands of visitors from all over the world – sailors and tourists – give Las Palmas an international atmosphere. The city has almost 100 hotels, but the number is decreasing, as many foreign tourists come to the somewhat loud and chaotic city for a day, but spend the rest of their holiday in Gran Canaria's sunny south.

> **! Baedeker TIP**
>
> **Harbour tour**
> Get to know Las Palmas from a completely different angle on a harbour tour: the *Bahia Cat* runs regularly from the Muelle Santa Catalina or the yacht harbour for an interesting tour. Information: tel. 928 24 99 22.

The city was founded on 24 June 1478 by **Juan Rejón**, who con- **History** quered Gran Canaria from here on the orders of the Spanish king. Since there were an unusually large number of palm trees in the place that the Spanish conquistadors had chosen for their administrative seat, it was named **Ciudad Real de las Palmas** (»royal city of the palms«). After the island was placed under Spanish rule in 1483 the time had come to move the bishop's seat from Lanzarote to Las Palmas in 1485. The town grew quickly. By 1487 about 3,500 people lived here; along with the Spanish there were many Genoese and Portuguese. The city profited from trade between Europe and the New World because of its location. Whether or not **Christopher Columbus** (►Famous People) really stopped on Gran Canaria in 1492, when he crossed the Atlantic for the first time, and stayed in Casa de Colón, which was named after him, has not been proven absolutely.

In the 16th century the city had to defend itself; it repelled attacks by the English, French and Portuguese seafarers again and again. The most difficult battle was probably in 1599 when the Dutch captain **van der Doez** tried to take Las Palmas with about 10,000 men. Las Palmas flourished in the 17th and 18th centuries. Beautiful buildings were built in the Vegueta district, some of which still exist. However, Las Palmas really took off when the port was established in the late 19th century. While only 16,000 people lived there in 1860, in 1900 there were already almost 50,000 residents. Las Palmas expanded in all directions; the old quarter Vegueta merged with Puerto de la Luz and many residential areas were established above the coast. When tourism began to grow in the 1950s a building boom began along Las Canteras beach. New hotels sprang up. Las Palmas has been the **capital of the island** since 1820. When the Canary Islands were divided into two provinces in 1927, Las Palmas became the capital of the eastern province Las Palmas de Gran Canaria. In 1994 a modern convention centre was built at the trade fair site.

← *A popular boulevard for strolling and shopping: Calle de Triana*

► VISITING LAS PALMAS

INFORMATION

Patronato de Turismo
Calle León y Castillo 17
Tel. 928 36 22 22
Fax 928 36 28 22

Information kiosks
In Parque San Telmo (opposite Ermita de San Telmo), at Paseo de las Canteras (opposite Hotel Meliá Las Palmas) and in Parque Santa Catalina.

PARKING

Parking in Las Palmas is extremely limited. It is best to go to one of the central parking garages in the old city at Teatro Pérez Galdós or in Santa Catalina district at the Edificio Elder.

BUS / TAXI

There are good express bus connections to the capital from the tourist centres in the south, as well as a good network of city buses. Line 1 runs back and forth every few minutes between Teatro Pérez Galdós and the port. From Parque de Santa Catalina an open tourist bus starts every 30 minutes on a city tour. For 8 euros you can get on and off as often as you want in one day.
Taxis are reasonable and there is probably no other city in Europe that has as many taxis as Las Palmas.

SECURITY

Las Palmas is considered to be the most dangerous city on the Canary Islands, but this doesn't mean that a robbery takes place on every street corner. During the day the city is no less safe than any central European city. At night it is best to be careful in the port district or Barrio Santa Catalina.

SHOPPING

Anyone who comes to Las Palmas to shop should go to Avenida de Mesa y López, where there are large department stores and branches of large shoe and fashion chains. Smaller boutiques can be found in the pedestrian zone Calle de Triana, which runs through the district of the same name. There are book and antique shops in the side streets. In Santa Catalina district electronics shops run by Indian immigrants sell watches, stereo equipment and computer equipment – it pays to compare prices.

Shopping centre El Muelle
At the harbour
Give in to your consumer instincts in the new shopping centre at the port. This modern retail paradise has diverse cafés and restaurants, cinemas and discos along with its more than 100 shops.

Mercado del Puerto
At the port, near Castillo de la Luz
Mon–Sat mornings
Groceries, clothing and souvenirs.

Mercado de las Palmas
Calle Mendizábal
Vegueta
Mon–Sat 8am–3pm
Fresh fruit, vegetables, fish and meat.

Flea market
Bus terminal
Near Parque San Telmo
Every Sunday morning.

FEDAC
Calle Domingo y Navarro 7
Not all of the crafts that are sold on Gran Canaria are actually produced there. The embroidery, basketry and

Las Palmas Map

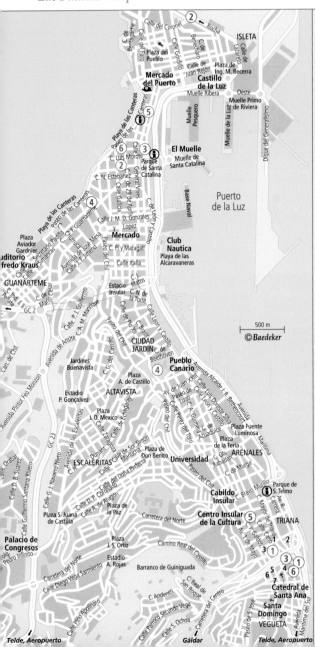

Where to stay
1. Madrid
2. Atlanta
3. AC Hotel
   Gran Canaria
4. Santa Catalina
5. Meliá
   Las Palmas
6. Reina Isabel

Where to eat
1. El Herreño
2. El Padrino
3. Hippocrates
4. El Novillo
   Precoz
5. Amaiur
6. Casa
   Montesdeoca

1 Casa Museo
  Pérez Galdós
2 Teatro Pérez
  Galdós
3 Gabinete
  Literario
4 Casa de Colón
5 Palacio
  Episcopal/
  Casa Regental
6 Casa Consistorial
7 Museo Canario

500 m

©Baedeker

wrought iron in the FEDAC shop are guaranteed to come from local workshops.

NIGHTLIFE

Venues

Especially around Parque de Santa Catalina or along the beach promenade there are bars, pubs and clubs.

Auditorio Alfredo Kraus
Paseo de las Canteras
Tel. 902 40 55 04
www.auditorio-alfredokraus.com
The best address for musical events from pop to classical.

Casino de las Palmas
In Hotel Santa Catalina
Calle León y Castillo 227
Tel. 928 23 39 08

www.casinolaspalmas.com
Roulette and Black Jack.

Pequeña Habana
Calle de Fernando Guanarteme 45
One of the most popular clubs in town; only Latino music. Hours: Fri–Sun 10pm–4am.

WHERE TO EAT

► **Inexpensive**

① *El Herreño*
Calle Medizábal 5
Tel. 928 31 05 13
Probably the best chance to try typical Canarian tapas and taste gofio. The traditional restaurant lives up to its name, »the man from El Hierro«, with wines and cheese from this little Canary island.

Market in Vegueta

El Herreño: perfect Canarian cuisine

② *El Padrino*
Calle J. Nazareno 1
(on Isleta)
Tel. 928 46 20 94
Simple restaurant with affordable prices and thus popular among the locals. How about shark steak or parrot fish?

③ *Hippocrates*
Calle Colón 4
Tel. 928 08 79 60
This little restaurant in the old quarter serves vegetarian food in simple surroundings. Most of the ingredients are organic
(closed Mon).

▶ Moderate
④ *El Novillo Precoz*
Calle Portugal 9
Tel. 928 22 16 59
There is no better grilled fish in Las Palmas than here. The many regulars have known this for a long time. The excellent quality has its price, of course, but you can choose the fish you want and also how you want it done: »a la brassa« (on charcoal), »a la ceniza« (in the ashes) or »a punta de llamas« (over flames). It is almost a sacrilege to eat the meat well done; the chef only recommends »a punto« (medium). Reservations recommended!

▶ Expensive

⑤ Amaiur
Calle Pérez Galdós 1
Tel. 928 37 07 17
One of the island's best restaurants, with suitably elegant atmosphere: bright, high rooms in an old townhouse. Basque cuisine is served midday and evening (closed Sun).

⑥ Casa Montesdeoca
Calle Montesdeoca 10
Tel. 928 33 34 66
Unique atmosphere: eat in one of the rooms of a wonderfully restored Canarian house or on the patio. Spanish cooking (closed Sun).

WHERE TO SLEEP

▶ Budget
① Madrid
Plaza de Cairasco 4
Tel. 928 36 06 64, fax 928 38 21 76
hotelmadridlaspalmas@telefonica.net
Half of the 40 simply furnished rooms have a shower and toilet; the ones without a bath are very reasonably priced. The hotel is appreciated mainly for its central location in the old city. The attached café-restaurant is also popular among non-residents.

▶ Mid-range
② Atlanta
Calle Alfredo L. Jones
Tel. and fax 928 26 50 62
www.atlantacanarias.com
This lower mid-range city hotel is in Santa Catalina district, about 50m/ 50yd from the beach. The 47 functionally furnished rooms and 20 apartments all have satellite TV, telephone and a safe. The central location means that it's not necessarily quiet!

③ Hotel AC Gran Canaria
Calle Eduardo Benot 3
Tel. 928 26 61 00, fax 928 22 91 39

www.ac-hoteles.com
This circular high-rise hotel dominates the tourist district Santa Catalina. It is 23 storeys high and thus offers a spectacular view from the upper floors, but the view can also be enjoyed from the roof terrace with a pool and the restaurant (see p.160).

▶ Luxury
④ Santa Catalina
Calle León y Castillo 227
Tel. 928 24 30 40, fax 928 24 27 64
www.hotelsantacatalina.com
The Spanish king stays in a suite in the Santa Catalina when he visits Gran Canaria. Other famous people like Plácido Domingo and Prince Charles have followed his lead. This typically Canarian house has been the city's top address since it opened in 1890. The terrace café under the hotel arcades offers colonial ambience, a 2,800 sq m/ 30,000 sq ft spa guarantees relaxation and a casino provides entertainment.

⑤ Meliá Las Palmas
Calle Gomera 6
Tel. 928 26 76 00, fax 928 26 84 11
www.solmelia.es
You can't help noticing that this hotel on the Playa de las Canteras has seen better times, but the 266 rooms and 46 suites are comfortable and live up to their five-star standard. There are also conference facilities, a swimming pool, restaurant and bar.

⑥ Reina Isabel
Calle Alfredo L. Jones 3
Tel. 928 26 01 00, fax 928 27 45 58
www.bullhotels.com
Five-star hotel on the beach promenade with 208 rooms and 16 suites. It has a large swimming pool on the roof terrace and several restaurants. The café terrace has a spectacular view of the sea.

Highlights *Las Palmas*

Museo Canario
The idol of Tara stands out in the leading Canarian collection.
▶ page 167

Playa de las Canteras
Stroll along the almost 3km/2mi-long promenade by one of the most beautiful beaches in the world.
▶ page 158

Vegueta
The old city with the cathedral and Columbus' house still emanates a colonial atmosphere.
▶ page 164

Parque de San Telmo
Take a break on the palm-shaded terrace of the beautifully tiled Art Nouveau café.
▶ page 161

City districts

Las Palmas' city districts all have a character of their own and there is no real city centre. The area around **Parque de Santa Catalina** and along Las Canteras beach is the most touristy area. The tall round Hotel AC Gran Canaria is the landmark of this district. Immediately to the east of Parque de Santa Catalina is the **port**, which has expanded to take in large parts of the Isleta.

Most of Las Palmas' attractions are in **Vegueta**, the oldest part of the city. Folk festivals and processions take place at Plaza de Santa Ana, its focal point. In the surrounding streets there are many beautiful old houses with artistic wooden balconies and quiet patios. To the north the district of **Triana** adjoins Vegueta. The pedestrian zone Calle de Triana with many shops is the centre.

Las Palmas' most luxurious district is **Ciudad Jardín** (»garden city«) at Parque Doramas. Many luxury villas are surrounded by lush gardens in the side streets of this district. The residents' fear of burglars is evident in the alarm systems and barred windows.

The **satellite towns** and the slums on the outskirts of Las Palmas stand in stark contrast to the exclusive Ciudad Jardín and the shopping districts with their extensive selection of goods. The city has grown in the past decades without any planning whatsoever. Depressing housing was built quickly to provide living quarters, but many people can't even afford to live in these grey dormer cities. The poorest of the poor live in slum-like squalor in huts of wood and corrugated iron, for example on Isleta. No wonder that crime in Las Palmas has grown dramatically (don't leave anything in your car!).

> ! **Baedeker TIP**
>
> **Bus or taxi**
>
> Longer distances in the town centre – from Castillo de la Luz at the port to Plaza de Santa Ana in the old city is about 6km/3.5mi – are best covered by public transport or taxi. Taxis are reasonably priced and probably no other city in Europe has as many taxis as Las Palmas. From Parque de Santa Catalina an open tourist bus starts every 30 minutes on a city tour. For 8 euros you can get on and off as often as you want in one day.

What to See in Las Palmas

Puerto de la Luz

Construction of the Puerto de la Luz, the port of light, began in the late 19th century; it was designed by the engineer **León y Castillo**. Puerto de la Luz has the sixth-largest turnover (7 million tons) of all Spanish ports, but in terms of traffic is even more important: about 14,000 ships call here every year. Ferries sail from the **Muelle de Santa Catalina** near Parque de Santa Catalina, transporting passengers and cars between the Canary Islands as well as to the Spanish mainland. Fishing boats dock here, too. But the actual fishing harbour is **Muelle Pesquero**. **Muelle de la Luz** is mainly used by freighters. **Dique del Generalísimo** is at the eastern edge of the port. Large tankers and cruise ships stop here.

Castillo de la Luz

Near Muelle Pesquero at Calle de Juan Rejón the Castillo de la Luz rises above green lawns. The small, almost square fort was built in the 16th century to protect the city from pirate raids. It was burned down in 1599 in the attack by van der Doez. Today it is used for cultural events.

Mercado del Puerto

Only a few hundred metres west of the fort on the way to Las Palmas beach stands the Mercado del Puerto, a 100-year-old market hall with an interesting iron construction.

Playa de las Canteras

Playa de las Canteras, one of the longest city beaches in the world, is more than 2.5km/1.5mi long and located in the north-west of Las Palmas. Its name (»canteras« means »quarry«) is a reminder that sandstone was taken from here for centuries for the cathedral of Santa Ana and other buildings. Reefs off Playa de las Canteras protect the beach from strong surf and make it possible to swim here safely. Considering its location the beach and the water are very clean: Playa de las Canteras was given a European Blue Flag award. It gets full on the weekends when thousands of local inhabitants come to relax on the beach. Playa de las Canteras is bordered by **Paseo de las Canteras**, a beach promenade with hotels, cafés, restaurants and shops. Island tourism began here in the 20th century.

Auditorio Alfredo Kraus

The **cultural and convention centre** at the south-west end of Playa de las Canteras is named after a native of Las Palmas, the tenor Alfredo Kraus (▶ Famous People). The imposing complex was built in 1997 to plans by the Catalan architect Oscar Tusquet. Imitating a medieval castle, the building stands out for its austere geometric ar-

It can get tight at weekends: Playa de Canteras

chitecture and is crowned by a small, round lighthouse. In the two concert halls, the Sala Sinfónica with 1,656 seats and the smaller Sala de Camára, about 100 concerts, from classical to pop and jazz, are held every year.

Parque de Santa Catalina

The centre of the tourist district in Las Palmas is Parque de Santa Catalina. On the shady pedestrian square there are several cafés, and street vendors sell their wares. Local people play chess and dominoes during the day, and in the evenings concerts often take place on an outdoor stage; the carnival queen is crowned here, too. The Casa del Turismo here has tourist information and brochures.

Museo Elder

Visitors to the **Science and Technology Museum** in Parque de Santa Catalina (Calle Emilio Castelar 6) can find out how glass is made, air traffic is controlled or ships are navigated. There are also historical exhibits, including a train from the year 1885 (hours: Tue–Sun 10am–8pm).

Hotel AC Gran Canaria	The circular Hotel AC Gran Canaria is the city's landmark and can be seen from far away. The panorama restaurant Le Volant (tel. 928 24 49 08) on the 23rd and 24th floors has the best view of the city.
✸ Parque Doramas	Take a taxi for the 2km/1¼mi between Parque de Santa Catalina and Parque Doramas. Walking through the drab streets clogged with traffic is not much fun. Parque Doramas is the centre of the high-class district called **Ciudad Jardín**. Wealthy Canarians live here in ostentatious villas set in lush gardens. Parque Doramas was named after the early Canarian king who ruled over the eastern part of the island. He was defeated in combat with the leader of the Spaniards, Pedro de Vera (► Arucas). With their leader gone, many of the early Canarians are said to have killed themselves by jumping off a cliff into a deep barranco. A modern monument on the eastern edge of the park commemorates

---

Baedeker TIP

Colourful folklore

The folklore show in Pueblo Canario (every Sunday at 11.30am) is performed for tourists, but it still gives an impression of the old dances and songs of the island – and the colourful costumes are delightful. The show is free.

---

this event. Typical Canarian flora grows in Parque Doramas, including several beautiful dragon trees. For children there is a small zoo in the northern part of the park.

Hotel Santa Catalina	Hotel Santa Catalina fits well into its surroundings. It is hard to believe that it was completed as recently as 1953. It replaced a hotel that was built by English investors in 1890 (see p.156).
Pueblo Canario	Pueblo Canario (Canarian village) was built next to Parque Doramas as an example of Canarian architecture. It was inspired by the water-colour paintings of the artist Néstor and begun in 1939. In the courtyard there are souvenir shops, the entrance to the Museum Néstor and a café. It is a refuge from the noise of the city.
Museo Néstor	Museo Néstor is located in Pueblo Canario. The museum was opened in 1956 and displays works of the Canarian painter Néstor Martín Fernández de la Torre (1887–1938; ► Famous People); the furnishings of his studio are also on display. Many of Torres' major works are strongly influenced by Symbolist art. In room 1 *Wedding Poem* and the self-portrait of Néstor de la Torre are among the most important works. The pictures in room 2 were made between 1934 and 1938 in order to provide models of typical Canarian architecture for the tourist industry. The paintings in room 3 all have the Atlantic Ocean as their theme; they were painted between 1913 and 1924. Room 4 is devoted to portraits, room 5 to drawings from 1934 to 1938, room 6 to sketches from 1913 on Mo-

zart's opera *Don Giovanni*. In room 7 there are sketches of decorations and costumes for various ballets; room 8 has some studies of plants. The pictures in room 9 are on the theme of *Earth*. Room 10 has drawings and sketches of Néstor de la Torres' main works from his whole life (hours: Tue–Sat 10am–8pm, Sun 10.30am–2.30pm)

To get to the **observation point** Altavista, leave Parque Doramas going west and cross Paseo de Chil, a broad thoroughfare; pass the monument to León y Castillo and keep going uphill to the west. The view from the observation point is reward enough: there is a wonderful panorama of Las Palmas and the ocean. (Careful! The area beyond Paseo de Chil is pretty rundown, and robberies are common here.)

Altavista

The southern extension of Calle de León y Castillo, Calle Mayor de **Triana**, is a **pedestrian zone** ideal for strolling. It is the main street of the area called Triana and has always been the city's business and shopping area. Art Nouveau buildings give the street its unique flair. Among the prettiest façades are **Casa Negrín**, which was designed by Fernando Navarro and built in 1907, and on the left **Casa Melián**, which was built a year later.

Calle Mayor de Triana runs past **Parque de San Telmo**. A tiled Art Nouveau pavilion from 1923, now a café, is a good place from which to watch the activity all around while seated under tall palm trees. The large building on the west side of the plaza houses the military headquarters of the Canaries. In this neo-classical building **General Franco** called for the deposition of the government in Madrid in 1936.

Art nouveau pavilion in Parque de San Telmo

The Ermita de San Telmo stands at the southern end of the park. The chapel was built in the late 17th century and dedicated to the patron saint of fishermen. Note especially the panelled ceiling inside

Ermita de San Telmo

in the Mudejar style. The many votive pictures in the chapel are mostly offerings from sailors who were spared from drowning at sea.

Museo Pérez Galdós

Calle Cano 6 – the street runs parallel to Calle Mayor de Triana – is the birthplace of the writer **Benito Pérez Galdós** (►Famous People). He was born in the house in 1843 and lived there as a boy. It is a typical 19th-century Canarian house with a picturesque courtyard. The **museum** that now occupies it has an interesting collection of works, Pérez Galdós' private library and a large number of personal items. In the study a life-sized wax figure of the poet is seated at the desk (hours: Mon–Fri 9am–9pm, Sat 9am–6pm, Sun 10am–3pm).

Plaza Cairasco

Plaza Cairasco in the south-west of Triana district is named after the poet Bartolomé Cairasco de Figueroa (1540–1610); his bust is in front of the Gabinete Literario described below. Mature trees, many benches, a sidewalk café and magnificent buildings around the square make Plaza Cairasco a charming place to rest in the bustle of Las Palmas.

Gabinete Literario

Gabinete Literario was built in 1842 as a theatre, but closed soon due to lack of funds. Only a few years later the Gabinete Literario, which

Las Palmas • Triana / Vegueta *Map*

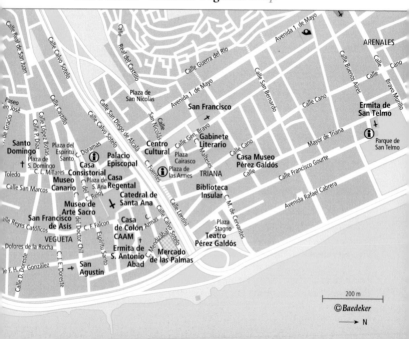

The Plaza Cairasco with a view of the illuminated façade of the Gabinete Literario is a good place to begin the evening

was founded in 1844, rented it. The city's oldest **cultural club** sponsors exhibitions and musical evenings, as well as publishing books. The building, which originally had a classical façade and was redecorated in the present style after World War II, was bought by the club in 1894 and is still used for cultural events.

Plaza de Cairasco is next to Plaza de San Francisco. Here stands the church Iglesia de San Francisco, which was built in the 17th century and expanded to three aisles in the 20th century. The Baroque main entrance dates from 1683. Inside note the Mudejar ceiling and several wooden statues by Luján Pérez. The most valuable work is a figure of Mary: the **Virgin of Solitude** (Virgen de la Soledad) is supposed to have the facial features of Isabella of Castille (1451–1504). It is possible that the queen herself gave the statue to the Franciscans.

Iglesia de San Francisco

Teatro de Pérez Galdós	East of Plaza de Cairasco, near the motorway that runs along the ocean, is the Teatro de Pérez Galdós, named after the famous novelist (►Famous People) who was a native of Las Palmas. The theatre was built in 1919 to plans by **Miguel Martín Fernández de la Torre**. The foyer is decorated with paintings by his brother Néstor de la Torre. The large hall seats 1,400 people. The theatre is generally only open for performances, from September to December. From January to April it is used for the music festival and opera festival.
Mercado de las Palmas	Cross Carretera del Centro to reach Vegueta, Las Palmas' oldest neighbourhood. Mercado de las Palmas, opposite the theatre to the south, is accordingly the oldest of the city's four market halls.

✳
Catedral de Santa Ana

Vegueta is dominated by Catedral de Santa Ana. Its interior and exterior show that construction took centuries. It began in 1497 and was interrupted in 1570, but the completed Gothic part of the church could already be used for worship. In the late 18th century and early 19th century the classical façade was completed by the sculptor **Luján Pérez** (1756–1815). He also built the three-storey north tower with its belfry and a small dome. The south tower was completed by 1857 as its counterpart.

The cathedral is divided into five aisles. Gothic ribbed vaulting is supported by slender columns. Valuable furnishings include a Baroque high altar as well as several works by Luján Pérez. The crypt has a monument to the Canarian poet and historian José de Viera y Clavijo (d. 1813). In the side chapels are the tombs of various famous islanders, including the engineer and port builder Fernando León y Castillo. The cathedral can only be viewed during services (Mon–Fri 8am–10am, Sat and Sun 8am–9.30am and 6pm–8pm) or via the Museo Diocesano de Arte Sacro.

> *Baedeker* TIP
>
> **Wonderful view**
> The climb to the newly constructed observation platform on the south tower of the cathedral is worthwhile (open: Mon–Fri 9.15am–6pm, Sat 9.15am–3pm).

Museo Diocesano de Arte Sacro	The Museo Diocesano de Arte Sacro is located in an aisle of the cathedral (entrance on Calle Espíritu Santo). Its treasures include statues, such as one by Luján Pérez, and a small picture gallery with the works of 16th-century Flemish painters as well as 17th- and 18th-century Canarian artists; it also has many gold and silver objects. From the Museo Diocesano de Arte Sacro it is possible to go into the quiet courtyard and the cathedral itself (hours: Mon–Fri 10am–5pm, Sat 10am–2pm).
Plaza de Santa Ana	The cathedral's main façade faces the palm-lined Plaza de Santa Ana. It is bordered by imposing administrative buildings and residences and by bronze **statues of dogs**, a reminder of the origins of the is-

Impressive: Catedral de Santa Ana on Plaza de Santa Ana

land's name (►p.15). However, the bronze figures have little in common with Canarian dogs, but were modelled on English dogs and set up about 100 years ago.

During the feast of Corpus Christi, Plaza de Santa Ana is decorated with a beautiful carpet of flowers.

Opposite the cathedral is the **city hall**, the Casa Consistorial. The main façade of the mid-19th century building is topped by a balustrade. Figures of early Canarians and Spaniards stand on the corner columns. The city coat of arms dominates the centre of the building.

Casa Consistori.

The military commander lives in Casa Regental next to the city hall on the north side of the square. It was built in the mid-17th century and a classical upper storey was added in 1805.

Casa Regental

A few metres further on the north side of the square is the bishop's palace (Palacio Episcopal). Only a Gothic entrance remains of the original 16th-century building.

Palacio Episcop

★ ★
Casa de Colón

Casa de Colón, near the back of the cathedral, was rebuilt in 1777 in typical Canarian style and was once the seat of the island's viceroy. It owes its name to **Columbus** (▶Famous People), who is supposed to have stayed in the previous building during a short stop on Gran Canaria. As part of the preparations for the 500th anniversary of the discovery of America in 1992, research was done. It emerged that, if Columbus stopped on Gran Canaria at all, he docked in the port of Las Palmas in order to repair the rudder on the *Pinta* in August 1492. It is certain, however, that Casa Colón is the birthplace of another famous person. A plaque on the wall of the house indicates that the opera tenor **Alfredo Kraus** (▶Famous People) was born here in 1927.

The attractive house with beautiful wood balconies and richly decorated stucco entrances now holds a museum (entrance on Calle Colón) with exhibitions on Pre-Columbian America; Columbus and his Travels; The Canary Islands as a Stage on the Way to the New World; and Origins and History of Las Palmas. A depiction of a cab-

Casa de Colón owes its name to Columbus – even though he never stayed here

in on Columbus' ship *La Niña* is especially interesting. The museum also displays paintings of the 17th to 19th centuries, most of which are on loan from the Museo Prado in Madrid. The two patios are pretty, the smaller one with a Gothic fountain (hours: Mon–Fri 9am–7pm, Sat, Sun 9am–3pm).

Ermita de San Antonio Abad

Columbus is supposed to have prayed in the Ermita de San Antonio Abad, located about 100m/100yd east of Casa de Colón, before setting off into the unknown. The chapel, the first Christian place of worship on the island, was built in the 15th century and completely restored in the 18th century.

Centro Atlántico de Arte Moderno (CAAM)

Only a few steps from Columbus' house in Calle de los Balcones 9/11 is the Atlantic Centre of Modern Art (Centro Atlántico de Arte Moderno, CAAM for short). While the façade is still original 18th-century work, the interior was completely restored in the 1980s. Exhibition rooms and offices on five storeys are grouped around a covered courtyard. This architectural style was intended to create a dialogue between traditional and modern styles. A collection of works by contemporary Canarian and Spanish artists is on display. There are also rotating exhibitions accompanied by courses and lectures.
For visitors there is also a library, videotheque and a collection of periodicals (hours: Tue–Sat 10am–9pm, Sun 10am–2pm).

★ ★ Museo Canario

Museo Canario, the pre-eminent museum on the islands, is located on Calle Dr. Verneau 2, south of Plaza de Santa Ana. It opened in 1880 and was completely reconstructed in the 1980s. It is a didactically well-conceived modern museum which gives excellent insights into the life and **culture of the early Canarians**; the archaeological finds and anthropological exhibits are supplemented by models and graphics. One room holds a model of living quarters with utensils and various ceramic articles of the early Canarians. On display are also more than 1,000 skulls (including some on which brain surgery was performed), numerous skeletons and some mummies. A reconstruction of the **necropolis of La Guancha** (►Gáldar) shows how the dead were interred. An exact replica of the **Cueva Pintada** of Gáldar has also been reproduced in the Museo Canario. Among the many items of ceramics, jewellery and utensils, the stone hand mills and the so-called pintaderas are noteworthy. The exact purpose of the pintaderas is still not known. Since no two of these wood or ceramic »stamps« are alike, it is assumed that they were used to make a personal mark on objects. The best-known early Canarian work of art is the **idol of Tara**. The 30cm/12in statue with grotesquely fat limbs appears female, even though it has no breasts.
The museum also has a reference library with about 40,000 books related to the Canary Islands or written by Canarian authors (hours: Mon–Fri 10am–8pm, Sat, Sun 10am–2pm; library: Mon–Fri 10am–8pm).

Generally a peaceful scene: the harbour of Las Palmas. Hotel AC Gran Canaria has a good view of the quay. The new shopping centre El Muelle is in the foreground.

THE DARKEST HOUR OF PUERTO DE LA LUZ

Every year about 14,000 ships call at Puerto de la Luz, the »harbour of light«. Fortunately there have been few accidents. Puerto de la Luz experienced the darkest day of its 100-year history just five years after being opened, when on 13 September 1888 the Italian passenger steamer *Sudamèrica* was rammed by another steamer while trying to enter the harbour and sank within minutes.

On this day at 5am three ships were approaching the harbour of Las Palmas from different directions: the 1,258-ton Italian passenger steamer *Sudamèrica* with 260 passengers and a crew of 69 on board, which had just crossed the Atlantic after visiting Buenos Aires and Montevideo; the steamer *La France* (4,600 tons) out of Marseille with 1,300 passengers, and finally the Spanish mail ship *Habana*.

Inevitable Collision

The *Sudamerica* appeared north of the city and then approached the harbour directly without reducing speed, while *La France* approached from the south heading straight for the Italian ship. Only the *Habana* had reduced speed and stayed away from the two steamers. The sea was calm, the sun rose slowly in the east and there was not a cloud in sight. But a collision was inevitable.

Panic on Board

The French ship rammed into the port side of the Italian ship with immense force. Woken by the massive collision, many passengers tried to get on deck even though they were hardly dressed. Panic soon spread when they realized that the steamer was sinking, and their cries mingled with the shrill ship's siren, which the crew of the *Sudamèrica* used to call for help. A few boats that were waiting nearby for the arrival of the *Habana* came immediately, but since these boats had no means of lifting the endangered passengers from the ship, many jumped from the deck. If they were lucky, sailors pulled them out of the water.

Help for a Few

Some passengers who did not manage to jump from the ship, or were afraid to do so, could no longer be helped. They were sucked under water by the vortex caused by the sinking ship. The passengers who were not able to get on deck suffered the same fate. However, the quick response of the small boats made it possible to save more than 250 people from drowning.

A few steps south of the museum on Plaza Santo Domingo stands the church of Santo Domingo. It dates from the 17th and 18th centuries, and is one of the most beautiful in Las Palmas. Note the magnificent Baroque altars and several statues by Luján Pérez inside.

Iglesia de Santo Domingo

Maspalomas

D 3

Maspalomas and Playa del Inglés together form the core of the Costa Canaria, the tourist region in southern Gran Canaria. The landmark of Maspalomas is its lighthouse, and the unique dunes to the east are one of the island's biggest attractions.

Unlike the bustling ►Playa del Inglés, Maspalomas is a quiet luxury-class holiday resort. Some of Gran Canaria's best hotel complexes and an exclusive golf course with every amenity are located here.

The dunes at Maspalomas are a leading attraction on the Costa Canaria

It all began in the 1960s west of the mouth of Barranco de Maspalomas, which runs through the developed area. Along with a handful of four-star and five-star hotels the most luxurious resorts on Gran Canaria are here, set in a magnificent grove of palm trees. Behind them are the **Campo de Golf** and **Campo Internacional**. Some of the complexes are not close to the beach, and try to compensate with a free shuttle service.

What to See in Maspalomas

★★
Dunas de Maspalomas

An area of massive **sand dunes**, the only one of its kind on the Canary Islands, extends to the south of the tourist city. It is a long time since they were an untouched landscape – there are footprints everywhere – but the high shifting sand dunes make an impressive picture with their wind-formed, pale yellow shapes.

The sand consists almost completely of carbonates and comes from the sea. The highest dunes, some reaching 10–20m (30–65ft), are closest to the water. Some of the dune valleys further inland have vegetation, but only a small part of the original dry growth has remained. Tourism has its price. In the late 1980s, however, Gran Canarians had a change of heart. Today 328ha/810 acres in the western part of the dunes are a nature reserve. Around the lagoon **Charca de Maspalomas** a new belt of sea grass is forming and many birds have discovered it as an ideal habitat, but the ecological balance in this area is still endangered.

★★
Playa de Maspalomas

The beach in front of the dunes is almost 4km/2.5mi long, from the mouth of Barranco de Maspalomas to Punta de Maspalomas, where it meets Playa del Inglés. This extensive beach is one of the most beautiful places for swimming on the Canary Islands. Paseo Marítima Oasis leads to Playa de Maspalomas. The Balneario Municipal here has showers, WCs and lockers. The only really busy part is the guarded section of beach by the hotels near the oasis. There is a **nude bathing zone** further to the east. Those who do not want to be disturbed retreat into the dunes.

Oasis de Maspalomas

The **Faro de Maspalomas** on the south-western edge of Maspalomas at the mouth of the barranco is the landmark of Oasis de Maspalomas. The lighthouse is 56m/184ft high and was the first building in this area. Its light can be seen for 25km/15mi. Oasis de Maspalomas is the most exclusive hotel area in the tourist city. Little has remained of the originally lush vegetation, except for what can be seen in the hotel gardens. A few palms have survived north of the hotels. **Paseo del Faro** runs parallel to the coast and is lined with restaurants and shops.

Maspalomas Map

Where to stay
1. Maspalomas Dunas
2. Bungalows Green Golf
3. IFA-Hotel Faro
4. Park and Sport Hotel Los Palmitos
5. Maspalomas Oasis
6. Palm Beach
7. Gran Hotel Costa Meloneras

Where to eat
1. El Labrador
2. Amaiur
3. Royal
4. L'Orangerie

▶ VISITING MASPALOMAS

INFORMATION

Tourist information in Playa del Inglés (▶p.182).

SHOPPING

The shopping centres Faro II and Varadero on the Costa Meloneras have a great variety of shops.

NIGHTLIFE

Maspalomas does not cater for nighthawks in the way that Playa del Inglés does. There is live music in the evening in Beethoven on the upper floor of Varadero shopping centre.

WHERE TO EAT

▶ Inexpensive

① *El Labrador*
Montaña la Data Alta
Towards Monte Leon
Tel. 928 14 12 88
Rustic restaurant with a terrace; also frequented by locals. Known for its grilled food.

▶ Moderate

② *Amaiur*
Avenida de Neckermann 42
Tel. 928 76 44 14
This Basque fish restaurant in Campo Golf has been established in Maspalomas for years. Come here for seafood with a view of the pool.

③ *Royal*
Shopping centre Faro 2
Campo Internacional
Tel. 928 76 94 80
Chinese cooking of the usual variety; friendly and quick service; there are tables on the terrace, too.

▶ Expensive

④ *L'Orangerie*
Avenide del Oasis

In the Palm Beach Hotel
Tel. 928 14 08 06
The best for ambience, service and food. Prices to match. The cuisine is French-inspired, the wine list simply excellent (hours: Mon, Wed, Fri and Sat from 7.30pm, reservations recommended).

WHERE TO SLEEP

▶ Budget

① *Maspalomas Dunas*
Avenida Jahn Reisen
Campo Internacional
Tel. 928 14 09 12
Fax 928 14 07 90
www.hotelesdunas.com
262 bungalows scattered through nicely planted, extensive grounds. The next main road is far away. The magnificent dune beach of Maspalomas is only 1km/0.5mi away and a shuttle bus runs three times a day. There are also three pools for sunbathers. The bungalows are functional.

② *Bungalows Green Golf*
Avenida Tjaereborg 2
Campo Internacional
Tel. 928 76 04 21, fax 928 76 74 09
Bungalow complex right next to the Maspalomas golf course. It is well suited for guests who want peace and quiet on their holiday. While each apartment is furnished for three people, they are not very spacious.

▶ Mid-range

③ *IFA-Hotel Faro*
Tel. 928 14 22 14, fax 928 14 19 40
www.ifa-hotels.de
The five-storey hotel at the Maspalomas lighthouse has bright and friendly rooms. The garden is quite small and there is not always enough room for all sunbathers.

④ *Park and Sports Hotel Los Palmitos*

Barranco de los Palmitos 22
Tel. 928 14 21 00, fax 928 14 11 14
www.lospalmitos.com
Located only 12km/7mi from Maspalomas, but it feels like a different world. 47 elegantly furnished rooms with terraces and a view of Palmitos Park. There are 6 tennis courts; individual lessons and courses available. Golf, horseback riding and hiking are also on the programme; there is also a spa and fitness centre.

► **Luxury**

⑤ *Maspalomas Oasis*

Plaza de las Palmeras
Tel. 928 14 14 48, fax 928 14 11 92
www.riu.com
The promise is in the name: this five-star hotel (local classification) of the RIU Group seems a bit like an oasis. The extensive park with old palm trees is open only to hotel guests. During the day residents meet at the large swimming pool or at the pool bar, in the evenings in the exquisite restaurant or for a drink at the bar; regular live music or shows.

⑥ *Palm Beach*

Avenida del Oasis
Tel. 928 14 08 06 ,fax 928 14 51 08
www.hotel-palm-beach.com
The seven-storey semicircular hotel is not very attractive from the outside, but after remodelling by the famous architect Alberto Pinto the interior is quite elegant. There is a new and luxurious spa area.

⑦ *Gran Hotel Costa Meloneras*

Calle Mar Mediterraneo 1
Tel. 928 12 81 00, fax 928 12 81 22
www.ghcmeloneras.com
The size, location and architecture of the Gran Hotel, which opened in 2001, make it an imposing example of the new hotel generation on the Canaries. It has 1,136 rooms and suites, five restaurants and a shopping arcade throughout 20 buildings on an area of 7.6ha/19 acres with several swimming pools. The extras include a large spa and a tennis school.

Gran Hotel Costa Meloneras

Campo Internacional	The area that borders the Maspalomas golf course on the north is called Campo Internacional. It consists of new bungalow settlements surrounded by green lawns. While the tourist centres and beach are a mile or two distant, many of the guests appreciate this very fact: the usual bustle is far away.
Holiday World	On the northern edge of Campo Internacional, Holiday World attracts young and old. The 1.4ha/3.5-acre site has a 27m/88ft Ferris wheel, a roller coaster, various carousels, scooter cars, a Mississippi paddle-wheeler on an artificial lake and parrot shows every evening. Tall palm trees, cacti and agaves as well as flowering plants, a biotope and fountains set create the scene, and restaurants and pubs offer refreshments and food (hours: Tue–Sun 6pm–1am).
Ocean Park, Aqua Sur	**Ocean Park** (hours: daily 10am–5pm, in the summer 6pm) at the north-east edge of Campo Internacional is a hit with kids. This alternative to the beach has a large pool area with waterslides, a wave pool and other attractions, but is not cheap. **Aqua Sur** (hours: daily 10am–5pm), north of the motorway on Carretera Los Palmitos, is even bigger and more expensive.

Around Maspalomas

osta Meloneras	The newest holiday area on the Costa Canaria is located west of Oasis de Maspalomas along the rocky **Playa de Meloneras**. Development of the unused area began in the mid-1990s. Riu Palace Meloneras, an attractive four-star hotel, lies right on the new promenade. The Gran Hotel Costa Meloneras with its exclusive spa is the flagship of the new resort area. There are already large up-market hotels and shopping centres nearby. Accommodation for a total of 7,000 guests is planned for the near future. The 900-seater **Auditorio Las Tirajanas** on Plaza de las Convenciones is the cultural centre of the Costa Meloneras.

Baedeker TIP

Casa de los Músicos

The pianist and conductor Justus Frantz has created a leafy paradise for himself in the hinterland of Maspalomas. The good news is that guests are welcome. The main house has two double rooms and two suites that can be reserved. Guests are welcome to use the sauna, pool and tennis court. The finca is located in the middle of an organic orchard and vineyard. Information and reservations: www.lascasascanarias.co.uk, tel. 0034/40/922 49 11 32

The stars for visitors to Palmitos Park

Pasito Blanco

West of Maspalomas a cul-de-sac runs to the **yacht harbour** Pasito Blanco 4km/2.5mi away. There is normally a barrier, but visitors are usually allowed to enter. A seaside promenade will soon connect Playa de Meloneras with Pasito Blanco.

El Tablero

El Tablero is located 4km/2.5mi north of the motorway, which forms a natural boundary to the tourist centres. This somewhat faceless village developed parallel to the growing tourism on the southern coast and is mainly a dormer village for the employees of the tourist industry.

Banana Park

On this finca in Barranco de Palmitos (access via the GC 503, turn left at km 6) you will learn about more than just bananas. Mangos, avocados, papayas and many other exotic plants flourish here as well. Children will love the donkeys, camels and ostriches (hours: daily 9.30am–5pm).

✶ ✶
Palmitos Park

Turn left just before the western edge of Maspalomas and follow the GC 503 north into the mountains to get to Palmitos Park (about 10km/6mi to Maspalomas). The gardens were planted in the 1970s in a steep-walled valley and have since grown to more than 20ha/49 acres. The park is home to 50 different varieties of palms, countless cacti and agaves. Along with a few gibbon monkeys there are about 230 species of birds. Ducks and swans swim on the pond in the centre of the park, and flamingos and peacocks strut around the lawns. The main attraction is the large number of parrots, some of which show off their talents in shows four times a day. Visitors can watch hundreds of butterflies from all over the world fly around the **butterfly house**. There is also an **aquarium** with fish from local waters as well as tropical fish and freshwater fish (hours: daily 10am–6pm; buses leave regularly for the park from various stops in Maspalomas, San Agustín and Puerto Rico; buses from Maspalomas run at least every 30 minutes).

Monte León Maspalomas' upper-class neighbourhood is Monte León, about 7km/ 4mi north-west of the centre. Of the many magnificent villas here, some belong to celebrities.

Mogán

C 2

Elevation: 250m/825ft above sea level   **Population:** 13,000 (entire district)

Mogán at the upper end of the barranco of the same name is the administrative seat of the coast between Arguineguín and Puerto de Mogán. The district is one of the richest in Gran Canaria because of the tax income that the tourist industry generates – even though Mogán was a remote mountain village until only a few years ago.

Baedeker TIP

Excursion into the interior

About 2km/1¼mi above Mogán a narrow road runs through remote, untouched mountain scenery to several reservoirs in the interior and then on to Ayacata (about 20km/12mi). There are also magnificent views back into the Barranco de Mogán. After countless curves and turns comes one of Gran Canaria's largest continuous pine forests. The relatively open forest extends from the Inagua (1,426m/4,678ft above sea level) in the west to Roque Nublo, the mountain in the clouds, in the east.

The village has only 700 residents and nestles at the foot of high mountains; it is bordered by fertile farmland divided into small fields. Thanks to the plentiful water supplies in the area, many residents have been able to make lush gardens around their cottages. Lemons, mangos, aubergines, papayas and other tropical fruits thrive here. Flowers are grown in hot-houses for export.

Several houses have signs outside indicating that they rent rooms or apartments.

► VISITING MOGÁN

WHERE TO EAT
► Inexpensive
Acaymo
Barrio del Tostador 14
Tel. 928 56 92 63
The trip is worthwhile: outstanding
Canarian food and a marvellous view
of the valley from the terrace (closed
Mon).

Meson Stephane
Town centre
Tel. 928 56 93 16

Homemade bread from a wood-
burning oven is also served. The
terrace seating is lovely. Closed Wed.

WHERE TO SLEEP
► Budget

Baedeker recommendation

Casa El Siroco
Calle San Antonio de Padua 8
Tel. and fax 928 56 93 01
www.costa-mogan.com/clients/siroco
This lovingly restored house in the centre of
the village near the church has simple bed &
breakfast accommodation. The four modest
rooms, two with bathrooms, are off the
patio. Ask for the tower room, whose
terrace has a beautiful view.

Around Mogán

From the main road that connects Mogán with ►San Nicolás de Tolentino, about 10km/6mi beyond Mogán there is a cliff that radiates
many colours. It is called Azulejos (»tiles«). Iron hydrate and other
iron compounds make the different shades of green in the rock.

Azulejos

Moya

B 3

Elevation: 488m/1,601ft above sea level   **Population:** 8,600 (entire district)

**Moya, the administrative centre of Moya district, is situated in the
foothills of the central mountain range about 30km/20mi west of
Las Palmas. The Canarian doctor and poet Tomás Morales
(1883–1921) was born here. Near Moya the remains of an original
laurel forest have been placed under strict protection.**

Moya is a pretty mountain village set on a rock plateau. The most
beautiful view of the town is from the GC 700, the road that connects Moya with Santa María de Guía. In the centre of the town the
parish church stands on a shady plaza.

What to See in Moya

Iglesia del Pilar The Iglesia del Pilar was built in the mid-20th century. It has fine statues of saints and woodcarvings. There is a wonderful view of Barranco de Moya from behind the church.

Museo Casa Morales The birthplace of **Tomás Morales**, which is right next to the church, now houses a small museum with Morales' private possessions and a library. The rooms are also used for public events. Morales spent his childhood and youth in Moya. He studied medicine in Cádiz and Madrid, and later worked as a doctor in Agaete. Morales' poetry describes the sea in lyrical verses. (Hours: Mon–Fri 9am–8pm, Sat 10am–2pm and 5pm–8pm, Sun 10am–2pm; free admission).

Around Moya

Tilos de Moya Most visitors come to Moya to visit the laurel woods (Los Tilos de Moya) in Barranco de Moya. At one time much of Gran Canaria was covered with woods like this one. To get there follow the main road from Moya towards Santa María de Guía. Turn off to the left at the sign »Los Tilos« and drive into the valley. On the valley floor the **laurel woods** border the road for about 200m/200yd. The dark green laurel leaves do not let much light through to the floor of the woods and there is a slightly musty odour. The surroundings hint at how lush the vegetation must have been here once.

San Bartolomé de Fontanales The narrow road winds through Tilos de Moya and on through **Barranco del Laurel** (»laurel tree«). At the upper end of the barranco the hamlet San Bartolomé de Fontanales lies in luxuriant greenery. This is one of the rainiest regions of Gran Canaria.

Playa del Inglés

D 3

Elevation: Sea level

Playa del Inglés and ►Maspalomas in southern Gran Canaria have merged and are by far the largest tourist area on the island. There are more tourist centres to the east and west; all of them together are called the Costa Canaria.

Playa del Inglés owes its popularity to the broad beach that stretches southwards for 4km/2.5mi to Punta de Maspalomas. The beaches can always be reached by bus from hotels that are further away. There is a good system of public transport on the **Costa Canaria**, and a drive to Las Palmas 50km/30mi away takes only about 30 minutes on the motorway.

Playa del Inglés Map

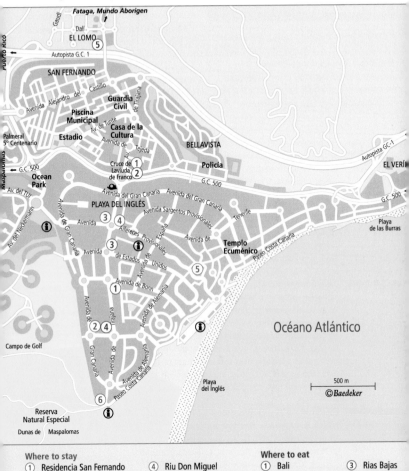

Where to stay
1. Residencia San Fernando
2. Sun Club
3. Aparthotel Barbacan
4. Riu Don Miguel
5. Seaside Sandy Beach
6. Riu Palace

Where to eat
1. Bali
2. Mesón Viuda de Franco
3. Rias Bajas
4. Tenderete II
5. La Casa Vieja

Don Alejandro del Castillo, Conde de la Vega Grande, the owner of   **History**
this otherwise unusable land, got the idea of building a holiday resort
there in the late 1950s. Until that time there was not even a fishing
village in the south and only one small paved road went there. But
the expansion soon began. The count, whose family tree went back
to Maciot de Béthencourt (▶History), founded various construction

Baedeker TIP

Sightseeing on a mini-train
About every half hour a replica of a miniature Western train from 1864 runs through the streets of the vacation centre (daily 10am–noon and 4pm–8pm). It is a good way to get a first or second impression of Playa del Inglés.

companies and gained a monopoly over the water supply. By the late 1960s his investment was beginning to pay off: tourists came in droves to the new hotels and apartments. Today Playa del Inglés and the surrounding communities have almost 150,000 hotel beds (the largest »tourist village« in Spain), and more are being added all the time.

Artificial holiday resort
At first glance it is evident that Playa del Inglés did not grow naturally. The city consists of nothing but large hotels, bungalow and apartment complexes, giant shopping centres, countless restaurants, cafés and discos – it could be anywhere. Depending on the season the broad four-lane roads and large roundabouts either hardly cope with the traffic or seem to be abandoned. In the small side streets of Playa del Inglés it is easy to get lost because all the hotel complexes surrounded by flower gardens look alike. The local people live to the north of Playa del Inglés in **San Fernando**. You either love Playa del Inglés or you can't stand it.

Playa del Inglés
The uncontested focal point of Playa del Inglés is the beach. The »English beach« is named after British holiday guests who came to Gran Canaria more than a hundred years ago looking for relaxation. However, they went to Las Palmas since the southern coast was completely uninhabited. Today German guests are in the majority, at least during the winter. On sunny days, of which there are on average 300 every year on the Costa Canaria, tens of thousands of people swarm over the 4km/2.5mi-long super-beach. It is fortunately up to 300m/1,000ft wide in some places.

Paseo Costa Canaria
In Playa del Inglés the Paseo Costa Canaria borders the beach. The **beach promenade** has a wonderful view of the dunes, especially in the evenings. Stroll along the Paseo Costa Canaria to the east as far as ▶San Agustín, to the west to Costa Meloneras.

Sports and fun
As would be expected of the largest tourist centre in Spain, the sports and entertainment attractions on the Costa Canaria are beyond measure. Equipment for all sorts of water sports can be rented at Playa del Inglés.

Around Playa del Inglés

✳ Mundo Aborigen
From Playa del Inglés drive north through San Fernando towards Fataga. The theme park and outdoor museum Mundo Aborigen is about 6km/3.5mi away. The park has an area of about 11ha/27 acres and depicts the everyday life of the early Canarian settlers. Simple

Playa del Inglés is not a lonely place when the weather is nice

stone round houses, the residence of the guanarteme (king), barns and workshops, burial grounds – in short, a complete **Guanche village** has been built here in replica. Life-size figures depict everyday scenes, such as men and women working in the fields, priestesses performing rituals and even a public execution. There is also a small archaeological museum with original finds. The park has a spectacular location with an excellent view of the breathtaking mountains and Barranco de Fataga from several vantage points (hours: daily 9am–6pm).

❯ VISITING PLAYA DEL INGLÉS

INFORMATION

Centro Insular de Turismo
Yumbo Center
Avenida España
Tel. 928 76 25 91
Hours: Mon–Fri 9am–9pm, Sat
9am–1pm

PUBLIC TRANSPORT

The communities of the Costa Canaria
are widely spread but connected by a
dense network of public transport.
Global bus company has an information office in the Yumbo Center.

SHOPPING

Shopping centres
There are several large shopping
centres, including Kasbah and Yumbo.
These shopping zones not only have
huge supermarkets, but also various
shops and above all many restaurants.
Prices can differ greatly from one shop
to another. Groceries are cheapest in
the supermarkets in San Fernando –
the locals shop here too.

Mercado
San Fernando

The Beckham Bar in Playa del Inglés is »in«

Shopping centre in the tourist city

The weekly market sells fresh groceries at relatively reasonable prices (Wed and Sat 8am–2pm).

NIGHTLIFE

Playa del Inglés is known all over the Canaries for its extravagant club scene. Nightlife is concentrated on the shopping centre Kasbah. The not-so-young crowd prefers the clubs in Centro Comerciales Cita. As the night advances the Yumbo Center turns into the largest gay venue of the Canary Islands. About 30 night bars, pubs, sex shops and dark rooms open on the upper floors.

WHERE TO EAT

▶ Inexpensive

① *Bali*
Avenida de Tirajana / corner of Avenida de Bonn
Tel. 928 76 32 61
This Indonesian restaurant is a good alternative to the usual international and Canarian cooking. The sate skewers with peanut sauce are a classic.

▶ Moderate

② *Mesón Viuda de Franco*
Cruce Viuda de Franco
San Fernando
Tel. 928 76 98 28
Unique restaurant in a former stable. The cooking is Canarian and international. Try the tapas at the bar or eat in the restaurant at affordable prices. The specialty is »vueltas de carne«, thin fillet of beef with lots of garlic.

③ *Rias Bajas*
Avenida Tirajana
Next to the Yumbo Center
Tel. 928 76 40 33
Popular among the local people. Fish and seafood is cooked Galician-style.

④ *Tenderete II*
Avenida de Tirajana
Tel. 928 76 14 60
Another place where not only tourists go. The atmosphere is both rustic and refined, and the food is Canarian. Try the »vieja«, a local fish similar to carp.

⑤ *La Casa Vieja*
On the road to Fataga
San Fernando
Tel. 928 76 27 36
Popular garden restaurant with specialties from the grill.

WHERE TO SLEEP
▶ Budget
① *Residencia San Fernando*
Calle La Palma 16
Tel. and fax 928 76 39 06
Don't expect much comfort or a good view in the cheapest accommodation on the Costa Canaria. This bed & breakfast is on the northern edge of town and has 60 clean rooms without ensuite bathrooms. Especially popular among young adults.

② *Sun Club*
Avenida de Francia 13
Tel. 928 76 28 70
Fax 928 76 28 78
sunclub@idecmet.com
Sun Club is one of the older holiday resorts with lush vegetation around 318 bungalows. The bungalows are quite spacious and have room for up to four people. They are reasonably priced when four people use them. The complex is divided into two parts by a road and has four tennis courts.

▶ Mid-range
③ *Aparthotel Barbacan*
Avenida Tirajana 97
Tel. 928 77 20 30
Fax 928 76 18 52
www.barbacan.es
The five-storey apartment building has an inner courtyard with flourishing plants and a pool. Some people will not like the location. Even though all rooms face the courtyard, the house is right in the middle of bustling Playa del Inglés, where the traffic noise has reached big-city level. The apartments are well equipped and have one or two bedrooms. The food in the restaurants is excellent, and the generous and varied breakfast buffet deserves a special mention.

④ *Riu Don Miguel*
Avenida Tirajana 36
Tel. 928 76 15 08
Fax 928 77 19 04
www.riu.com
Could not be more central, but could be quieter! Most of the balconies face the courtyard with two swimming pools. A bus runs to the beach and back regularly. Rooms can only be reserved with half-board.

⑤ *Seaside Sandy Beach*
Calle Los Menceyes 1
Tel. 928 77 27 26, fax 928 77 40 08
www.seaside-hotels.com
A good place for parents, but not only for families. Playground, children's programmes and professional child-minding are available. The 256 rooms are furnished suitably and have balconies and marble bathrooms.

▶ Luxury
⑥ *Riu Palace*
Plaza de Fuerteventura 1
Tel. 928 76 95 00, fax 928 76 98 00
www.riu.com
Riu Palace offers the best view of the dunes in Maspalomas. The rooms have luxurious bathrooms. The garden is a good place to relax. Both tennis courts have floodlights and the house also has a gym and a beautiful sauna area.

✶ ✶ Pozo de las Nieves

C 3

Elevation: 1,949m/3,094ft above sea level

Gran Canaria's highest mountain, Pozo de las Nieves (»snow well«) or Pico de las Nieves (»snow peak«), is in the centre of the island. Snow lies on the mountain for only a few days a year – and then only for a short time.

The peak of Pozo de las Nieves, where there are radar and TV antennae, is easy to reach on three roads that start at Cruz de Tejeda near Ayacata or in Telde. Coming from Ayacata drive past **Presa de los Hornos**, the highest reservoir on the island at 1,550m/5,085ft, then turn off right towards Telde. After 3km/2mi comes the turnoff to the right to Pozo de las Nieves. The road leads past a military zone to the **observation point**, which has a marvellous view of ►Roque Nublo. About 2km/1¼mi further to the east – also accessible by car – there is another observation point.

Snow well

At the fork to the two observation points a »snow well« (Pozo de las Nieves) from 1699 was reconstructed. The island residents used to fill the shaft, which is 10m/33ft deep and 5–7m/16–23ft wide, with compressed snow in the winter. The ice remained until summer and was then transported to Las Palmas, where it was used for cooling during hospital operations, for example. There used to be three snow wells around the peak.

✶ Puerto de las Nieves

B 2

Elevation: Sea level   **Population:** 800

The approach to Puerto de las Nieves on the road along the west coast commands a grand panorama of the town at the foot of the cliffs. The »snowy port« has two landmarks: the rock needle Deo de Dios and a chapel dedicated to the »Virgin of the Snow«.

North-west ferry port

Puerto de las Nieves was once a major port. Agricultural products from the region were loaded here; ships running between Las Palmas (Gran Canaria) and Santa Cruz (Tenerife) mostly called at Puerto de las Nieves as well. Then the port slumbered for decades. Today it is a port of call for **passenger and car ferries** that connect Puerto de las Nieves (Agaete) with Santa Cruz de Tenerife several times a day (duration approx. 1 hour). There is a new yacht harbour, and colourful fishing boats bob in the water.

Puerto de las Nieves has developed into a small tourist attraction in just a few years. There are apartment complexes around the centre of town. A pretty **promenade** runs from the port along the small beach and is an inviting place to stroll.

Foreign tourists still only come for a short stopover. At weekends, when local people come to the many excellent fish restaurants, it can be difficult to find parking in Puerto de las Nieves.

What to See in Puerto de las Nieves

Ermita de la Virgen de las Nieves

The Ermita de la Virgen de las Nieves is located on the main road in a walled compound. The brilliant white chapel is worth a visit, especially for the triptych attributed to the Flemish painter Joos van Cleve (d. 1541). It was brought to Gran Canaria in the 16th century. The centre panel depicts the Virgin with child sitting under a canopy. During the **Bajada de la Rama** (4–7 August) the altar painting is carried from the chapel to the parish church of Agaete in a procession joined by most of the local population. The beautiful Mudejar ceiling of the chapel is also worth seeing. The model ships displayed along the walls are offerings from sailors for the Virgen de las Nieves, the Virgin of the Snow.

At the Bajada de la Rama in front of the Ermita de la Virgen de las Nieves

⏵ VISITING PUERTO DE LAS NIEVES

INFORMATION

Oficina de
Información Turística
Calle Nuestra Señora de las Nieves 1
Tel. 928 55 43 82

WHERE TO EAT

▶ **Inexpensive**
El Dedo de Dios
At the harbour
Tel. 928 89 80 00
Typical Canarian establishment with a
huge picture window offering a view
of the sea. Specialty: seafood of all
kinds.

▶ **Moderate**
La Palmita
On the Puerto de las Nieves –
Agaete road
Tel. 928 89 87 04
Comfortable restaurant with a pretty
terrace; many day-trippers come here
at weekends. There is a playground
for young guests.

WHERE TO STAY

> *Baedeker recommendation*

▶ **Mid-range**
Puerto de las Nieves
Avenida Alcalde José de Armas
Tel. 928 88 62 56
Fax 928 88 62 57
www.hotelpuertodelasnieves.net
A comfortable four-star hotel, one of the
few with a high standard in the almost
tourist-free north-west Gran Canaria. It is
located at the edge of town and has 30
rooms furnished in a modern style. The spa
with indoor pool, sauna, massages and
various other therapies is attractive.

A few hundred metres south of Puerto de las Nieves, **Dedo de Dios**
(»finger of God«) juts out of the sea close to the coast. This 30m/
100ft-high monolith has an unusual shape; its point broke off during
a violent storm in late 2005.

✶✶ Puerto de Mogán

Elevation: Sea level   **Population:** 1,000

**Puerto de Mogán is the western outpost of the southern tourist
centre of Gran Canaria. The small town is located at the mouth of
Barranco de Mogán (▶Mogán), one of the most fertile valleys on
the island. While in the 1980s only a few fishermen lived here with
their families, Puerto de Mogán has developed at breakneck speed
in the last twenty years. Now the centre of town is made up of exclusive housing and an elegant yacht harbour.**

VISITING PUERTO DE MOGÁN

SHOPPING

Mercado
Most of the day guests come on Friday for the market that is held between 8am and 2pm around the port.

BOAT TOURS

The »Yellow Submarine« starts from the port every 40 minutes to explore the undersea world (which is not very impressive in this area!). Boat trips along the natural coast west of Puerto de Mogán, on the other hand, are very pleasant. Choose between sailing or deep-sea fishing (experienced person-nel help beginners). If that is too much trouble, take one of the local ships into the neighbouring towns of Puerto Rico or Arguineguín.

WHERE TO EAT

▶ Moderate

Bodeguilla Juanana
Promenade at the harbour
Tel. 928 56 50 44
Rustic restaurant; the seats are old wine barrels and the decor is in flea-market style. A good place to try Canarian specialties, but seafood is quite expensive!.

Tu Casa
Avenida de las Artes
Tel. 928 56 50 78
This pretty old house with terrace right on the beach has good Italian cuisine.

Baedeker TIP

Diving

Puerto de Mogán is a centre for diving on Gran Canaria. A range of courses are organized by Atlantik Diving at Hotel Club de Mar (www.hotelpuertodemogan.com; tel. 89 35 20 49).

Baedeker recommendation

▶ Expensive

La Caracola
At the harbour, tel. 928 56 54 86
The »Seashell« is one of Gran Canaria's gourmet establishments and has prices to match! As the name indicates, the restaurant is known for its fish; shark and swordfish are served in many tasty variations. With only 20 seats, reservations are an absolute must (closed from May to late July).

WHERE TO STAY

▶ Mid-range

Taurito Princess
Urbanización Taurito
Tel. 928 56 54 00, fax 928 56 55 66
www.princess-hotels.com
This all-inclusive resort has all the comforts expected of a hotel in this category. All 400 rooms have an ocean view. The huge seawater pool in the middle of lush green grounds is a special attraction (non-guests may use it for an admission charge).

Club de Mar
Tel. 928 56 50 66, fax 928 56 54 38
www.clubdemar.com
The two-storey house is attractive for its Mogán-style architecture and situa-tion right on the yacht harbour. The bright rooms all have a view of the sea or the port. Steps from the swimming pool lead directly into the sea. The hotel also has several apartments, some with two bedrooms.

▶ Budget

Pensión Lumy
Lomo Quiebre 35, tel. 928 56 52 35
A simple backpacker's hostel with ten basic but clean rooms.

Puerto de Mogán is very stylish. Two-storey white cottages with colourful door and window frames line the traffic-free lanes. Abundant floral decoration, pretty squares and many cafés and restaurants make it an inviting place to relax and shop. Gran Canaria is proud of its »Little Venice« since the whole community has shown that efforts are being made to get away from the negative aspects of mass tourism. Many visitors leave without having explored the old part of Puerto de Mogán. By all means take the time to do so: whitewashed houses and cobbled streets bring the past to life.

★ ★
Little Venice

The 400m/450yd-long Playa de Mogán next to the holiday resort is made of light sand. A wave break ensures safe swimming for children but restricts the water circulation.

Playa de Mogá

This part of Puerto de Mogán is located 1km/0.5mi into the barranco from the beach; it existed long before tourism came. The modest houses now house bed & breakfast accommodation for the backpacking crowd.

Lomo Quiebre

Puerto de Mogán: Gran Canaria's model tourist resort

Around Puerto de Mogán

aya del Taurito 4km/2.5mi to the east, Playa del Taurito (or Playa del Diablo) is also surrounded by tourist resorts. There is a large pool area with palm trees, flowers and water slides in the centre (admission charge for non-residents).

Playa de Veneguera Playa de Veneguera is a small beach with dark sand and stones west of Puerto de Mogán. Access is only on foot on a traffic-free road. By car drive via Mogán and Casas de Veneguera (25km/15mi one way). At Playa de Veneguera another development with 20,000 beds is planned, but environmentalists have succeeded in delaying construction.

★★
Playa de Güigüí The region's and possibly the island's most beautiful beach, Playa de Güigüí, is located further west (►Baedeker Special, p.192).

Puerto Rico

Elevation: Sea level   **Population:** 1,000

Puerto Rico on the south-west coast of Gran Canaria is completely oriented to tourists. Those who come here are less interested in entertainment than in sports. Puerto Rico has two yacht harbours, and almost everything revolves around water sports here.

Puerto Rico, the »rich port«, was built in a sheltered bay that is bordered by 100m/330ft cliffs. The apartment buildings climb up the cliffs almost to the top. With about 30,000 beds Puerto Rico is the **second-largest tourist centre** on Gran Canaria.

At first glance it might be difficult to imagine taking a vacation here, but a second look reveals many green oases that relieve the overall impression of concrete. There is one disadvantage: when the weather is good the small, artificial beach is full to overflowing and swimmers, sailors and surfers have to be careful to avoid collisions.

Aguapark Aguapark on the northern edge of town provides fun in the water for the whole family. The main attractions are the waterslides and
⊙ the kamikaze tunnel (hours: daily 10am–6pm).

Around Puerto Rico

★
Playa de los Amadores Puerto Rico is connected to the very upmarket Playa de los Amadores to the north-west by a panoramic promenade. The 400m/450yd-long curved beach is considered to be the most beautiful on the island. It was only constructed a few years ago and is made of

Puerto Rico Map

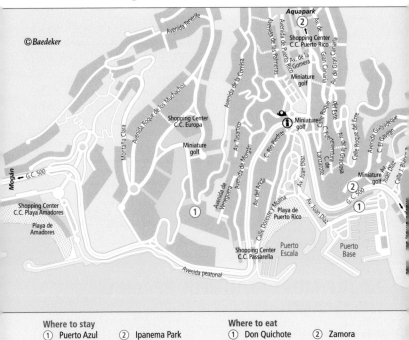

©Baedeker

Where to stay
① Puerto Azul   ② Ipanema Park

Where to eat
① Don Quichote   ② Zamora

white sand. Jetties built into the sea protect the beach from surf and make it ideal for children. Above Playa de los Amadores a new exclusive holiday resort is being built into the cliffs.

Playa de Tauro is located about 4km/2.5mi north-west of Puerto Rico (turn left after the campgrounds). The beach is about 400m/450yd long. The eastern part is the most attractive. **Playa de Tauro**

In the bay next to Tauro lies the Beach Hotel Riviera on a beach that is jam-packed during the high season. **Playa de Cura**

The next beach, Playa del Medio Almud, is accessible only on foot and is the preferred beach of the Canarians (a road turns off the coast road at km 78). While the beach is not very clean, the beach parties here are quite festive. However, the untouched setting will soon be gone: excavators are already on the march. The adjacent **Playa de Tritaña** has not yet been discovered by developers. A footpath begins at the coast road and runs 600m/650yd to the narrow beach of fine-grained sand. **Playa del Medio Almud**

TO THE MOST BEAUTIFUL BEACH ON THE ISLAND

Many people think that Playa de Güigüí on the west coast is the loveliest beach on Gran Canaria. Since parts of this beautiful coastal landscape are a protected natural area, it will be saved from tourist development, at least in the near future. Playa de Güigüí is only accessible by boat or on foot, after a strenuous hike.

Those who opt for the **boat** can get a yacht or fishing boat to take them to the beach from Puerto de Mogán. The price is negotiable but will not be less then 75 euros. Remember that there is no jetty, so you will have to either swim ashore or take an inflatable dinghy.

A Strenuous Hike

The 12km/7mi tour starts at the hamlet **Tasartico**, which is only accessible by car. Allow at least five hours for the hike to the beach and back. There is a difference in elevation of 970m/3,200ft (round trip). The hiking trail is steep in parts, slippery and goes over gravel paths. There is no shade! Make sure you take enough water ...! It is only possible to get from E1 Puerto Bay to the larger Playa de Güigüí at low tide. The local newspapers list the times of the tides (bajamar = low tide, pleamar = high tide). Make sure that you allow enough time to get back to El Puerto during low tide. The way between the two bays is cut off at the onset of high tide. Until the tide turns again there is no way back ...!

Only for experienced hikers: the hike to Playa de Güigüí

Off We Go

The hike starts at the hamlet Tasartico in the barranco of the same name. A few houses are gathered around a small church. Follow the path that continues from the paved road into the barranco. Vegetables are grown in the valley, some in greenhouses. After about ten minutes go right after a greenhouse and follow the path, which is easy to recognize, uphill. The dry vegetation on the slope includes tabaiba and euphorbia. After a few turns the path leads into the side barranco Cañada de Aguas Sabinas. After 15 minutes cross the floor of the barranco to the left. The path now runs uphill. It is long, steep and quite strenuous, in some places paved with stones and in others covered with loose gravel. The climb takes some time and finally arrives at a small marble cross and then the pass. This is the lowest part of the mountain ridge that divides Barranco de Tasartico and Barranco de Güigüí Grande. From here there is a wonderful view of wild mountain landscape with the blue, sparkling ocean in the background. The sound of surf can be heard from far off. After a break, begin the descent. The old path is in better shape here and the far-off destination beckons already. The path winds in places, and sometimes runs straight downhill. After about 45 minutes there is a fork in the trail: one branch leads straight ahead along the slope; follow the other path to the left into the barranco (a small farm can be seen further down). In about ten minutes you will reach the valley floor. Follow the rocky rubble downhill – not the path, which soon turns off to the right. Walk under a pipeline that crosses the barranco. Soon after go left along a path into Barranco de Güigüí Grande and follow the valley. The rubble here is densely covered with Spanish cane; walk downhill on the right of the rubble and pass along the lower border of a small farm. A partially sandy path leads down into **El Puerto Bay** via steps cut into the rock; Barranco de Güigüí Grande opens up into the sea here.

The Lure of the Beach

At low tide walk along the beach to the right into the sandy **Playa de Güigüí**; Barranco de Güigüí Chico runs into the sea here. Since this way is never completely dry, even during low tide, take your shoes off here to walk around the protruding rocks. Remember to return before the tide turns …! Follow the same route back, which now includes a strenuous hike uphill.

This text originally appeared in German in the Kompass hiking guide *Gran Canaria*.

VISITING PUERTO RICO

INFORMATION

Oficina de Turismo
Avenida de Mogán
Tel. 928 56 00 29

BOAT TOURS

Regular ship traffic (Lineas Salmon) connects Puerto Rico with Puerto de Mogán and Arguineguín. One way takes about 30 minutes. The ships run several times a day. Aquarium Cat is a glass-bottomed catamaran that lets passengers see the undersea world. Tours in a sailing boat or catamaran are also attractive.

NIGHTLIFE

Nightlife is limited in Puerto Rico. The restaurant El Pirata on the promenade has live bands several times a week; sometimes there is a flamenco show. Young people go to the clubs in the Centro Comercial.

WHERE TO EAT

► **Moderate**

① **Don Quichote**
Edificio Porto Novo 12
Tel. 928 56 09 01
This restaurant right on the harbour serves fish, seafood, paella and flambé

It may not be pretty but the view is good: holiday accommodation at Playa de Tauro

meat dishes. Porcelain plates on the walls commemorate Don Quichote, the »Knight of the Woeful Countenance«. Very popular, reservations recommended (closed Sun and Mon).

② *Zamora*
2km/1¼mi outside town on the road into Barranco de Puerto Rico
Tel. 928 56 05 17
In the part of town where the local people live; only open in the evening. Good Spanish and Canarian cooking at reasonable prices (closed Sun).

WHERE TO STAY
► Budget
① *Puerto Azul*
Cornisa Puerto Rico
Tel. 928 56 05 91
Fax 928 56 10 28
www.hotelpuertoazul.net
The hotel is not right on the beach, but a shuttle service brings guests to the beach in a few minutes. The rooms are very spacious and all have a roomy terrace with a view of the ocean. There is also a kitchenette for self-catering. A swimming pool, two

tennis courts, a playground and entertainment keep the guests occupied.

② *Ipanema Park*
Barranco Agua la Perra
Tel. and fax 928 56 03 00
E-mail: ollaes@sadocon.com
The 114 apartments are modern and furnished functionally; above all there is a wonderful view over Puerto Rico bay. The walk to the beach is long and includes lots of steps. A bus runs to the town centre several times a day.

► Mid-range
Gloria Palace Amadores
Avenida de la Cornisa
Tel. 928 12 85 10
Fax 928 12 85 14
www.hotelgloriapalace.com
This four-star hotel dominates Playa de los Amadores. A lift brings guests to the promenade, from which the walk to Puerto Rico takes 10 minutes and to Playa de los Amadores 15 minutes. The rooms are attractive; there is a miniclub and playground for children.

✶✶ Roque Nublo

C 3

Elevation: 1,813m/6,000ft above sea level

Roque Nublo, the »rock in the clouds«, is at the centre of Gran Canaria only a few miles west of Pozo de las Nieves. It is considered to be the island's landmark because of its unusual shape.

Roque Nublo is a monolith that rises 80m/260ft over a mesa. The remarkable »needle rock« was once part of an even higher mesa and is all that remains after erosion. The rock was sacred to the Guanches.

Roque Nublo is located in romantically untouched landscape and only accessible on foot. The short **hike** (about 4km/2.5mi round trip,

Ascent

Spectacular view of Roque Nublo

150m/500ft climb) starts at a parking lot on the road that connects Ayacata and Cueva Grande. There is a path from the parking lot to the rock, which is already visible. The »rock in the clouds« often lives up to its name. The best time to be sure to see it in sunlight is early in the morning.

San Agustín

D 3

Elevation: Sea level

San Agustín, a hotel city in southern Gran Canaria, borders ►Playa del Inglés to the west, but the atmosphere here is more refined than in the nearby tourist centre.

San Agustín does not have a town centre. Hotels and other tourist facilities dominate the scene, but the many little lush and blooming gardens make it colourful. The GC 500 runs through the middle of San Agustín. Anyone who is staying north of it can get to the beach via pedestrian bridges.

Take the time to stroll along the beach promenade (Playa del Inglés is about 4km/2.5mi to the west), which follows **Playa de San Agustín**, a 600m/650yd-long beach that is considered to be one of the best-kept on the island. On the east is Punta Morro Besudo, a rock promontory that protects the beach from the north-east winds. The waves in the cove are generally low and the gently shelved beach is safe for children as well.

Around San Agustín

The Playa de San Agustín is bordered on the east by small sandy coves. The 500m/550yd-long, but somewhat stony **Playa del Águila** is very pretty. It merges with **Playa de Tarajalillo**. The latter is part of the community Bahía Feliz (Happy Bay), a comfortable Moorish-style holiday village and at present the easternmost part of the Costa Canaria. Scandinavians and windsurfers stay in this quiet community. The well-known Club Mistral has a surfing station here.

Bahía Feliz

Just a few miles north-west of San Agustín a replica **Western town** has been built in Barranco de Aguila. Sioux City with its saloons, church, bank, jail and other buildings has been used as a setting for television shows. There are shows several times a day with lasso and duelling stunts, knife-throwing etc. (hours: Tue–Sun 10am–5pm).

Sioux City

Drive 10km/6mi north-east from San Agustín to **Juan Grande** and then on to the fishing village of Castillo del Romeral. The name comes from a fortress that no longer exists; it was built to protect the nearby salt works. Fishing boats bob in the water along the jetty; there is a seawater pool instead of a beach. The Cofradía de Pescadores next to the little harbour serves reasonable fish dishes; the selection depends on what was caught that day.

Castillo del Romeral

The average tourist is not likely to have heard of this small coastal settlement 16km/10mi north-east of **San Agustín**, but it is one of the sweetest-sounding names in the world in the ears of windsurfers. This section of coast has hardly been developed and is one of the best places in the islands for strong winds. A world cup race for surfing

Pozo Izquierdc

VISITING SAN AGUSTÍN

Baedeker TIP

Gran Canaria from the air

For a bird's eye view, try a ride in a helicopter. They are available at Aerodrom El Berrial near San Agustín (approx. 30 minutes): Blue Canarias Helicopters, tel. 28 77 47 48, www.bluecanarias.com.

NIGHTLIFE

Casino

In Hotel Meliá Tamarindos
Roulette and blackjack daily between 8pm and 4am. There is also a hall of slot machines.

Show in the Casino Palace

Calle Las Retamas 3
Tel. 928 76 27 24
www.casino-palace.net
Every evening in the Casino Palace opposite the casino an extravagant dinner show is performed (choice of menu, gourmet menu and vegetarian menu).

WHERE TO EAT

▶ Inexpensive

Loopy's Tavern
Calle Las Retamas 7
Tel. 928 76 28 92
International cuisine (chicken, pizza, steaks etc.) all day long. The modest restaurant is popular with families.

▶ Moderate

El Puente
Calle las Dalias 3
Tel. 679 77 10 36
This restaurant is only open in the evening and has a fabulous view of the coast. Closed Mon.

WHERE TO STAY

▶ Luxury

Meliá Tamarindos
Calle Retama 3
Tel. 928 76 26 00, fax 928 76 22 64
www.solmelia.com
It is obvious at a glance that this seven-storey five-star hotel, whose tower can be seen from far off, was built in the 1970s. The rooms are a bit small but of the usual standard in this category. The range of evening entertainment is a great plus; there is a classy revue and the casino attracts guests from the entire area.

▶ Mid-range

Dunas Don Gregory
Tel. 928 77 38 77, fax 928 44 53 20
www.hotelesdunas.com
The nine-storey, 250-room Don Gregory is also not very attractive on the outside, but the location is great: only the promenade separates the hotel from the beach. The maisonette apartments in the eighth floor are more spacious than the standard rooms.

pros has been held here every summer for years. The only facilities worth mentioning are two surfing bars, a handful of the simplest guest houses as well as the public Centro Internacional de Windsurf-ing (CIW), where windsurfing and diving courses are offered mainly for local people.

Nearby are the island's wind-power facilities and a salt works.

San Nicolás de Tolentino

C 2

Elevation: 64m/210ft above sea level   **Population:** 10,000 (entire district)

San Nicolás de Tolentino lies in a fertile valley where many of the residents still live from agriculture. The water supply comes from several reservoirs in the interior, where the trade winds bring rain. Tomatoes, potatoes, bananas, papayas, avocados and mangos are grown.

Located in western Gran Canaria, 5km/3mi from the coast, San Nicolás de Tolentino is still relatively difficult to reach. In the past the harbour, Puerto de la Aldea, was almost the only means of contact with the outside world.

San Nicolás de Tolentino is an elongated village without a real centre. Between the whitewashed houses there are still a few windmills to pump groundwater to the surface, but the water has become too salty for most plants.

Around San Nicolás de Tolentino

San Nicolás de Tolentino does not have much to attract visitors. A stop in Puerto de San Nicolás or **Puerto de la Aldea** is more interesting. This still quite rustic **fishing village** has a few simple restaurants that serve the seafood catch of the day. The good value they seem to offer is the only explanation for the many local guests at weekends. The **beach** near Puerto de San Nicolás is about 500m/550yd long, relatively stony and bordered by cliffs. Expect strong waves. Most of the visitors are anglers.

Puerto de San Nicolás

Drive through the Barranco de la Aldea to get one of the most beautiful scenic impressions of Gran Canaria. Although the road is well surfaced, it is very narrow and winding (!); it runs eastwards through the barranco from San Nicolás.

At first it passes farms and fields, then several reservoirs surrounded by steep cliffs. After about 20km/12mi the mountain road meets the road that connects ► Artenara and Pinar de Tamadaba. Since the

★
Barranco de la Aldea

> ! **Baedeker TIP**
>
> ### Fun in the mud
>
> On 10 September San Nicolás de Tolentino celebrates the Fiesta del Charco, the »pond festival«. It goes back to the year 1766. The bishop at that time came for a visit and arrive at a bad moment: he caught men and women swimming almost naked in the pond. That coul not go unpunished and the whole village was excommunicated. Today the festival is more decent: no-one swims naked, but everyone has great time! There is also a contest at some poin the person who catches the most fish in the pond wins.

road is not used much, it is good for mountain bikers as well, but they should bear in mind that the differences in elevation along the route amount to about 1,300m/4,300ft.

The lower part of the barranco, around today's San Nicolás, was among the most popular settlement areas in pre-Hispanic times. Many ceramic finds and remains of early Canarian walls were discovered here. The individual sites are not marked and hard to find without an experienced guide.

Cactualdea   Cactualdea lies on the road to Mogán, about 4km/2.5mi south-east of San Nicolás de Tolentino. As the name already hints, it's all about **cacti**. About 100,000 plants grow on the grounds, where there are also reconstructed Guanche caves and an amphitheatre where **lucha canaria**, Canarian wrestling, is demonstrated. Small cacti are sold in a souvenir shop and a restaurant serves refreshment (hours: daily 10am–6pm).

noramic coast   The drive to the west coast is a worthwhile experience. The best part of the GC 200 runs from San Nicolás de Tolentino to Agaete. The most spectacular stops are **Mirador de Balcón** and **Anden Verde**, two observation points with a marvellous panorama of the wild and romantic coast.

Santa Brígida

Elevation: 509m/1,650ft above sea level   **Population:** 18,000 (entire district)

Santa Brígida, a healthy 15km/9mi south-west of Las Palmas, is the capital's upper-class suburb. The elevation means it is always a bit cooler than Las Palmas, and the pretty scenery has made it the community of the rich and successful on the island.

The area around Santa Brígida and Tafira is Gran Canaria's **main wine growing region**. »Vino del Monte« is considered to be the island's best red wine. It is available in local bars and restaurants.

The houses in Santa Brígida are scattered over hillsides, and some of the villas have large gardens. Tall eucalyptus trees give the village atmosphere.

Around Santa Brígida

La Atalaya   The village of La Atalaya, about 5km/3mi south-east of Santa Brígida, is known for its **pottery**. However, hardly any of it is still made in the old style without using a potter's wheel. Since the village is a stop-off for many island bus tours, most of the potteries have gone over to mass production.

⏵ VISITING SANTA BRÍGIDA

SHOPPING

There is a flea market and art market in the Parque Municipal every Saturday morning, where bargains are still to be had.

WHERE TO EAT

▶ Expensive

Las Grutas de Artiles
In Las Meleguinas
Tel. 928 64 05 75
This restaurant has existed for decades in Santa Brígida. It serves excellent Canarian food; the desserts are especially tempting. The restaurant is located in several caves, which gives it a unique atmosphere.

▶ Moderate

El Martell
El Madroñal
On the road to Vega de San Mateo
Tel. 928 64 12 83
A typical Canarian restaurant with rustic furnishings. Wide selection of Canarian wines, including local red wine. It is full at weekends, so reservations are a must (hours: daily noon–5pm and 8pm–midnight).

WHERE TO STAY

▶ Mid-range

Santa Brígida
Calle Real de Coello 2
Monte Letiscal
Tel. 928 35 55 11
Fax 828 01 04 01
www.hecansa.com
The Santa Brígida has a long tradition: it opened its doors in 1898. Today it is associated with the state school of hotel management. This means that the staff are very motivated and friendly, if not yet perfect! For the guests in the 41 double rooms, there are the obligatory swimming pool, gym and conference facilities.

Baedeker recommendation

Villa del Monte
Calle Castaño Bajo 9
Tel. 928 64 43 89
Fax 928 64 15 88
www.hotelvilladelmonte.com
This finca with seven rooms is situated in wonderful garden at an elevation of 800m 2,600ft. The rooms are all furnished individually, and a three-course meal is available in the evenings upon request. A pretty place not just for mountain bikers and hikers!

Good wines come from the area around Santa Brigi

Some of the residents on the edge of town still live in caves, but most of the caves are no longer recognizable as such since they have conventional house façades. They are furnished with modern appliances and comfortable furniture.

Santa Lucía

C 3

Elevation: 701m/2,800ft above sea level   **Population:** 45,000 (entire district)

Santa Lucía is only a few miles east of Tunte (San Bartolomé de Tirajana), also on the edge of the Caldera de Tirajana. The picturesque village is a popular stop on island tours. The mosque-like dome of the church in Santa Lucía can be seen from far off. White houses and palm trees are clustered around it.

What to See in Santa Lucía

The museum near Restaurant Hao, **Museo Castillo de la Fortaleza**, is the village's main attraction (about 50m/50yd from the main road; follow the signs). The »pseudo-castle« displays fossils and household articles of the Guanches. One room is furnished in typical 17th-century Canarian style. The special treasures of the carefully designed private collection include a Roman amphora from the 3rd century AD; it was found on the ocean floor near Lanzarote. A few old cannon are on display in the garden next to the museum and restaurant (hours: daily 9am–3pm).

Around Santa Lucía

Fortaleza Grande or **Ansite** is a group of peaks south of Santa Lucía that were sacred to the Guanches. Coming from Santa Lucía, turn off the GC 65 to the right 2km/1¼mi outside town towards La Sorrueda. After driving through the hamlet set in a palm grove, a large open area appears after another 3km/2mi. A path runs from here about 100m/100yd to the cave entrance in Fortaleza Grande. Walk 20m/65ft through the cave to another entry.

In April 1483 the early Canarians hid here during the Spanish conquest. Only their former guanarteme, Tenesor Semidan, who had already converted to Christianity, could convince the 1,600 men, women and children to give up

►taleza Grande

SANTA LUCÍA

WHERE TO EAT

► Inexpensive

Hao
Tel. 928 79 80 07
The proprietor of the museum also owns the rustic garden restaurant Hao (bus tours welcome!). Try the delicious papas arrugadas with mojo sauce, but also stewed rabbit or grilled kid.

and let Spanish forces take over Gran Canaria (►Gáldar). Ceremonies are held every year on 29 April on the assembly ground below the cave to commemorate this event.

Santa María de Guía

B 3

Elevation: 186m/610ft above sea level   **Population:** 14,000 (entire district)

Santa María de Guía, Guía for short, is next to ►Gáldar in northwestern Gran Canaria. When stopping here on the way to Cenobio de Valerón, be sure to taste the delightful »queso de flor« that is produced in Guía.

Guía was established in the late 15th century as a suburb of Gáldar. Recent Spanish immigrants settled here. Guía became an independent town in 1526. The streets of Santa María de Guía are full of life. The parish church (Iglesia de la Asunción) has neo-classical elements. Some of the statues inside – Nuestra Señora de las Mercedes is the most important – are by Luján Pérez (1756–1815), who was born in Guía and whose statues of saints can be found in all major churches in the archipelago.

> ! **Baedeker** TIP
>
> ### Don't miss it!
> Guía is known for its queso de flor. This cheese i made of sheep's milk and sap extracted from artichoke blossoms – hence the name. The sap gives the cheese an especially aromatic taste and also keeps it soft over a long period. The »flora cheese« is available in many shops in Guía (lik Santiago Gil, Calle Marqués del Muni 34, near the municipal park), but also in farmers' market and the market halls of Las Palmas.

Queso de flor: artichoke flowers create the unique aroma

Tafira

Elevation: 300 – 400m/1,000 – 1,300ft above sea level **Population:** 3,000 (entire district)

Tafira, about 8km/5mi south-west of Las Palmas, just like ► Santa Brígida, is a well-to-do suburb of the capital. It is divided into two parts: Tafira Baja and Tafira Alta. A visit to Tafira is worthwhile because of the Jardín Canario.

Tafira stretches for 3km/2mi along the four-lane road from Las Palmas to Vega de San Mateo. The houses show that the owners are wealthy.

Around Tafira

★ ★
Jardín Canario

Jardín Canario (Canarian Garden; officially Jardín Botánico Canario Viera y Clavijo) is located in the community of **La Calzada**, below Tafira Alta. The public gardens have two entrances. One is on the road from Las Palmas to Santa Brígida (GC 15), the other on the Tamaraceite – Santa Brígida road (GC 308). The park extends into the Barranco de Guiniguada, along the valley floor and up the eastern slope. Many small paths and steps crisscross the grounds (to avoid the steps use the entrance on the Tamaraceite – Santa Brígida road).

Jardín Canario was founded in 1952 by the Swedish botanist Eric R. Sventenius; it has been open to the public since 1959. Its name commemorates **José de Viera y Clavijo** (1731–1813), who wrote a *Lexicon of Canarian Natural History*.

The plants in the park are all natives of the Canary Isles or other Macaronesian Islands (endemic plants). The garden was planned to be like the native habitat of the plants and is a complete success: in the extensive grounds palm trees, laurel and dragon tree groves alternate with broad lawns and smaller plant beds. Many of the plants that can be seen here are difficult to find in their natural habitat. The cultivation of these plants is intended to prevent their extinction.

A large collection of succulents with rare varieties from Africa, Central and South America is attached to the park. In central and north-

> **TAFIRA**

WHERE TO EAT

► Moderate

Restaurante Jardín Canario
Carretera de las Palmas
Tel. 928 43 09 39
The restaurant is located at the upper entrance to Jardín Canario. Along with its good Canarian and international cooking it is known for its marvellous view of the park (hours: daily noon–4pm and 8pm–11.30pm).

Winding paths lead through the Jardín Canario

ern Europe they only grow in hothouses and then only as small plants; in Jardín Canario some have grown to a considerable size. The luxuriant vegetation and the generous water supply have attracted a wide variety of birds to the park. Canaries, goldfinches and Tenerife robins, to name a few, can be heard here (hours: daily ⏀ 9am–6pm; free admission).

★ Tejeda

C 3

Elevation: 1,049m/3,400ft above sea level

Population: 2,600 (entire district)

Almost every tourist on Gran Canaria drives through the village of Tejeda in the centre of the island at least once. It has a picturesque location between the mountains and is a popular photo motif, but not very many tourists stop here; most of the tour buses stop at the highest point of the pass, the ►Cruz de Tejeda.

Always good for a picture: Tejeda

The village of Tejeda has no special attractions, but its location makes a visit worthwhile. The **almond blossom** in late February is the best time to visit. A large almond blossom festival is held then, the exact date depending on the blossoming time; tourist offices have information.

Around Tejeda

The 1,412m/4,633ft **Roque Bentaiga** towers over Tejeda. To get there drive 4km/2.5mi on the main road from Tejeda southwards and turn off to the right (signposted). After 500m/550yd keep left. Follow the trail on the right from the parking lot of the Centro Interpretación Roque Bentaiga (closed most of the time). It soon becomes rocky and leads up to the plateau below the basalt monolith. From there steps chiselled into the rock lead up to a Guanche religious site. The Roque de Bentaiga was sacred to them. They met here for sacrificial ceremonies (there are basins chi-

WHERE TO EAT

▶ **Inexpensive**

Labrador

Tel. 928 66 60 45

The simple village restaurant opposite the church feels duty-bound to cook in Canarian style. The favourite is rabbit with lots of garlic. There is outdoor seating in fair weather.

selled into the rock for libations) and festivals that lasted several days. They probably stayed in caves during these festivals; the entrances can still be seen on the slopes.

A particularly large cave (11m/36ft long, 7m/23ft wide and 2.50m/8ft high) west of Roque de Bentaiga and above the hamlet El Roque is called **Cueva del Rey** (king's cave). There are basins in the floor of the cave similar to those at the foot of Roque de Bentaiga. There are no signs to mark the cave – ask a local resident for help.

A very winding and narrow lane leads from El Roque to the hamlets of **La Solana** and **El Chorillo**. The picturesque valley with terraced fields and small orchards is one of the most untouched parts of Gran Canaria.

El Chorillo and the neighbouring hamlet of El Carrizal are connected by a path. From the end of the road in El Chorillo climb the steps into the village and follow the old paved path up to a wooden cross. There is a wonderful panoramic view of Mesa de Acusa from the path. The last part of the way to El Carrizal is on a trail. After a refreshment at one of the two bars in El Carrizal follow the same trail back (round trip about 2 hours).

Hike from El Chorillo to El Carrizal

> ## Baedeker TIP
>
> ### Sweet things
>
> In Tejeda the Dulcería Nublo (Calle Dr. Hernández Guerra 15) is a popular stop for those with a »sweet tooth«. The little pastry shop sells local specialties made of almonds and marzipan. Try the piñones or pan de batatas, made of sweet potatoes.

Telde

B/C 4

Elevation: 116m/382ft above sea level   **Population:** 89,000 (entire district)

Telde, 15km/9mi south of Las Palmas, is the second-largest city on Gran Canaria. Various industries have settled around Telde. But there is still a certain amount of agriculture; citrus fruits and sugar cane are the primary crops.

The edge of town is characterized by large shopping centres, warehouses and factories. In the bustling centre the streets are usually jam-packed. Barrio San Francisco in the north and Barrio Los Llanos in the south of Telde are the oldest parts of town. The genteel citizens lived in San Francisco, while Los Llanos was the neighbourhood of the black slaves who worked on the sugar cane plantations. It is not surprising then that **San Francisco** with its narrow streets and attractive houses is considered to be a fine example of an old Canarian town.

Begin a tour of this quarter at Plaza de San Juan and its church, which is bordered by pretty old houses. Follow the lane up to Plaza de San Francisco, where time seems to have stood still. Until the Franciscans were expelled in 1836, the little church was their home.

Telde can look back on a long history. This area was the seat of the guanarteme who ruled the eastern part of the island in early Canarian times. The many pottery shards that have been found here and the reports of the Italian Leonardo Torriani indicate that the area was densely populated. The villages of Tara and Cendro were located here. Tara is known as the site where the most famous ancient Canarian work of art, the idol of Tara (see p. 38), was found. After the Spanish conquest the cultivation of sugar cane and the sale of sugar were the main sources of income. Telde was also known for its slave market.

What to See in Telde

The Iglesia de San Juan Bautista

Iglesia de San Juan Bautista, in the northern part of Telde, is worth a visit. It was built from volcanic stone of different colours beginning in 1520. The 16th-century Gothic main façade survives. Changes were made in the 17th and 18th centuries; the nave was renovated in the 19th century. The two bell towers were added in the 20th century.

Inside the church, which is dedicated to John the Baptist, the Flemish **retable** dates from around 1500. The artistic carving depicts six scenes from the life of the Virgin. The main picture (top centre) shows the birth of Christ; other scenes show Mary and Joseph's wedding, the annunciation by the archangel Gabriel, Mary visiting Elizabeth, the circumcision of the baby Jesus and the adoration of the Magi. Above the altar there is a **statue of Christ** from Mexico. The life-size 16th-century figure weighs only 7kg/15lbs because it was made from the pith of corn plants. Other art treasures in the church include a depiction of St Bernard by Vicente Carducci (1578–1638) as well as some sculptures by Luján Pérez.

▶ **TELDE**

INFORMATION

Oficina de Turismo
Plaza de San Juan 2
Tel. 928 13 90 55

WHERE TO EAT

▶ **Inexpensive**
Bar Alameda
Plaza de San Juan 12
Tel. 928 68 51 08
The little bar vis-à-vis the church serves Canarian stew.

Museo León y Castillo

There is a small museum in Telde dedicated to the brothers Fernando ▶ Famous People and Juan León y Castillo (Calle León y Castillo 43–45). Fernando was a government minister in Madrid who did much for his island home. The large port in Las Palmas was his idea. His brother Juan was born in this house in 1843 and carried out his brother's project. The typically Canarian house with a wooden balcony has furniture and memorabilia inside; pictures and plans of the harbour are on display in the courtyard (hours: Mon–Fri 8am–8pm, Sat, Sun 10am–1pm).

Around Telde

Montaña de las Cuatro Puertas (»mountain of the four gates«; 319m/1,060ft above sea level) is about 5km/3mi south of Telde on the road to Ingenio. Four openings have been carved into the peak, which is accessible by car up to 200m/660ft. They lead to a chamber that was used by the early Canarians as a religious site. The area in front of the cave served as a **tagoror**, an assembly ground. On the south slope of the mountain there are more Guanche residential caves, some of which are natural while others were hewn out of the rock. Steps can be seen that were carved into the floors of some of the caves.

Montaña de las Cuatro Puertas

Iglesia de San Juan Bautista has numerous art treasures

✷✷ Teror

B 3

Elevation: 543m/1,781ft above sea level   **Population:** 13,000 (entire district)

Teror is considered to be the most typically Canarian town on the island. In the centre, note the old houses with artistic wooden balconies and beautiful patios; some of them are decorated with coats of arms. The Sunday market is an attraction.

The statue of the Virgen del Pino, the patron saint of Gran Canaria, is kept in the basilica. On 8 September every year the Fiesta de Virgen del Pino is the island's biggest festival, attended by Canarians from far and wide.

What to See in Teror

✷✷
Basílica de Nuestra Señora del Pino

The most important building in Teror is the Basílica de Nuestra Señora del Pino. It was built on the site where the Virgin Mary is supposed to have appeared to some shepherds. According to legend the »miracle« took place on 8 September 1481. The shepherds saw the mother of God in the branches of a giant pine tree, which was

Altarpiece in the Basílica de Nuestra Señora del Pino

knocked over in a storm in 1684. Juan Frías, the first bishop of the Canaries, must have found the vision very convenient since it gave the Christianization of the island a significant impetus. A chapel was built on the site on his orders and replaced in 1692 by a larger church. This one was almost completely destroyed in an explosion in 1718; only the tower survived. It is integrated into the present basilica, which in turn was built between 1760 and 1767.

The 1m/3ft-high statue of the **Virgen del Pino** survived the explosion of 1718 undamaged. The 15th-century statue stands in a silver palanquin that was made in the 18th century in La Laguna (Tenerife). The two halves of the virgin's face have different expressions. One half appears to be suffering, while the other half is smiling softly. Those who want to see this can climb the stairs in the back of the church to see the figure up close (open: Mon–Fri 2pm–6pm, Sun 10.30am–2pm and 3.30pm–6pm). The Virgen del Pino was named the patron of the island by the pope only in 1914. Until then the Virgen de la Candelaria, the patron of Tenerife, was also the protector of Gran Canaria. In 1929 the Virgen del Pino received military honours: King Alfonso XIII declared her to be Capitan General. During the feast day, along with sacred and folk music, military marches take place and soldiers salute the statue. Another valuable relic in the basilica is a cross that was carved from the legendary pine tree; it is kept under glass.

VISITING TEROR

INFORMATION

Oficina de Turismo
Calle Padre Cueto 2
Tel. 928 61 36 09

SHOPPING

Sunday market
There is a market every Sunday morning around the basilica. It sells delicious and very fresh groceries; inspecting the rummage and the craft items is also fun.

WHERE TO EAT

► Moderate
El Secuestro
Avenida Cabildo Insular
Tel. 928 63 02 31
Grilled meat, rustic setting. The restaurant is only open Thu–Sun; it is full at the weekends!

Mirador de Zamora
On the GC 21, 1km/0.5mi before Valleseco
Tel. 928 61 80 42
At weekends it is hard to get a table at this popular panorama restaurant. The menu includes classics of Canarian cuisine like rabbit or hearty potaje (stew).

WHERE TO SLEEP

► Budget
Cortijo San Isidro
San Isidro
Reservations via Turismo Rural
Tel. 928 39 01 69, fax 928 39 01 70
www.ecoturismocanaraias.com
Three fully furnished holiday apartments for four or five people can be rented in this carefully restored country house.

The main event on the island: Fiesta de la Virgen del Pino

Casa Museo de os Patrones de la Virgen

Diagonally opposite Casa Museo de los Patrones de la Virgen (Plaza Nuestra Señora del Pino 3) there is a well-preserved example of Canarian architecture. The house was built around 1600 and was the summer residence of the Manrique de Lara family, the patrons of the Virgen del Pino. Today it houses a museum (hours: Mon–Thu 11am–6pm, Sun 10.30am–2pm). The many exhibits (paintings, weapons, dishes etc.) and the pretty patio give an attractive impression of life on the Canaries in the past centuries.

Georg Hedrich studio

The museum also exhibits some works of the German painter Georg Hedrich. He has lived on Gran Canaria since 1957 and has his studio and gallery near the church (Plaza Nuestra Señora del Pino; hours: Tue, Wed, Thu 11am–3.30pm).

Plaza Teresa de Bolívar

The little plaza next to the church is named after Teresa de Bolívar, the wife of the leader of the Latin American freedom movement, **Simón de Bolivar** (1783–1830). There is a bust of the Venezuelan freedom fighter on the square. Teresa's great-grandfather is said to have been born in Casa de los Patrones.

Around Teror

Valleseco

The road from Teror to the village of Valleseco 8km/5mi to the west is very winding. The name »dry valley« is confusing since the area is very fertile. Potatoes, fruits and vegetables are grown. The village is located at an altitude of 950m/3,000ft above sea level and dominated by the white, Moorish-style parish church.

The observation point half a mile before Valleseco has the best view
of Teror and the over-populated northern mountains. At exactly the
right place there is a large tourist restaurant that is completely over-
run at weekends.

Balcón de Zamora

Tunte (San Bartolomé de Tirajana)

C 3

Elevation: 887m/2,910ft above sea level   **Population:** 40,000 (entire district)

**Tunte or San Bartolomé de Tirajana, as it was called until a few
years ago, is located on the edge of the Caldera de Tirajana, which
borders the central mountains on the south. It is a good place to
start exploring the mountains even though it has no sights and
hardly any tourist infrastructure.**

Tunte – the name is early Canarian – is the capital of the district of
San Bartolomé de Tirajana, with 334 sq km/129 sq mi the largest
municipio on Gran Canaria. Since
the district includes the tourist
centres Maspalomas, Playa del Inglés and San Agustín, the administration has expanded in the past
decades. The population of the district has grown rapidly from only
about 9,000 in 1950.
Only about 3,500 people live in the
town itself today, and Tunte still
has the character of an untouched
mountain village. The mainstay of the local economy is fruit (al-
monds, plums, apricots and cherries), which is mainly used to make
liquors and cordials. »Guindilla«, the sour cherry cordial made here,
is a specialty.

> **? DID YOU KNOW ...?**
>
> ■ »Caldera« is the geological term for a crater
> that has been widened by collapsing walls o
> erosion, but there is no indication that
> Caldera de Tirajana has volcanic origins. The
> semicircle was probably formed by massive
> landslides.

What to See in Tunte

The church is dedicated to St James (»Santiago«), the Spanish patron
saint. The Mudejar ceiling and several statues of saints inside the
18th-century building are worth seeing.

Iglesia de Santiago

Around Tunte

To explore the Caldera de Tirajana, the semicircular valley bordered
by mountains north of Tunte, drive north on the GC 60 and turn off
after 2km/1¼mi onto a side road to the east, which has beautiful
views. Pass the settlements of Agualalente, La Culata and **Risco Blanco** (»white rock«). The latter gets its name from the brilliant white

Caldera de Tirajana

Pretty cottages decorated with flowers abound in Tunte

cliffs in the area. After driving through Taidia and continuing for a good 10km/6mi you will meet the GC 65, which connects Santa Lucía with Tunte.

balse de Chira From the GC 60 7km/4mi north-west of Tunte a road turns off left to the Chira reservoir. Avoid it at weekends because of the many day-trippers. The first stop is the hamlet **Los Cercados**. Jeeps can follow the unpaved road along the southern shore of the reservoir. The Finca El Oso right on the shore serves refreshments. A road winds southwards from the end of Embalse de Chira and ends up in Playa del Inglés.

Ayacata Ayacata is located 10km/6mi north-west of Tunte in a picturesque valley surrounded by high cliffs. Major tourist routes branch off here to Pozo de las Nieves and the reservoirs Cueva de las Niñas and Soria; many holiday-makers use the chance to take a break in a restaurant here.

Hike from Cruz Grande to Pico de las Nieves From Tunte take the GC 60 towards Tejeda; after just 5km/3mi you will reach Cruz Grande at 1,250m/4,101ft elevation. The striking gorge is the starting point of a spectacular mountain hiking tour up to **Degollada de los Gatos** (»Cat Pass«) and on to Pico de las Nieves. 50m before the gorge the sign »Riscos de Tirajana« marks the beginning of the trail. Soon a breathtaking path winds up the cliff in tight serpentines to the pass. At a dip in the trail after just two hours, follow the path to the right that is marked by little stone men to the Degollada de los Gatos only a few minutes away. To continue follow the ridge trail another 45 minutes toward the two radar domes on Pico de las Nieves up to Mirador Pico de las Nieves (altitude 1,940m/6,365ft). Allow five to six hours for the somewhat strenuous round trip. You can get to the starting point Cruz Grande from Maspalomas by bus.

Vega de San Mateo

B 3

Elevation: 836m/2,743ft above sea level   **Population:** 7,000 (entire district)

Vega de San Mateo is a typical mountain village, located a good 20km/12mi south-west of Las Palmas. Most people just call it San Mateo. The livestock market on Sunday is the big attraction.

Goats, pigs, cows and small animals change hands at the market. Cheese products, vegetables and fruit are also for sale. The products all come from the immediate area, since the good water supply makes agriculture possible here.

What to See in Vega de San Mateo

Iglesia de San Mateo has a statue of St Matthew, the patron of farmers and cattlemen, dating from 1652.

Iglesia de San Mateo

The Museo Etnográfico La Cantonera is housed in five farmhouses – one thought to have been built in the 16th century – on the plaza. The museum exhibits old household utensils and agricultural implements from past centuries. The museum has a restaurant.

Museo La Cantonera

INDEX

LIST OF MAPS AND ILLUSTRATIONS

PHOTO CREDITS

Borowski: p.34, 115 (right, left above), 117 (right below)
CMA: p.92
dpa/Picture Alliance: p.26, 27, 45, 52, 55
Fan & Mross/Friedel: p.1, 59
Fan & Mross/R. Müller: p.7, 50, 117 (left below)
Fan & Mross/Hackenberg: p.65
HB/Widmann: p.4 (left below), 21 (right above, left and right below), 42, 72, 81, 95, 111 (centre), 123, 140, 145, 150, 161, 166
HB/Zaglitsch: p.3 (left below), 9, 12 (above), 36, 39, 48, 64, 107 (right above), 111 (left above, below), 113 (left), 117 (left and right above), 120/121, 128, 131, 132, 134, 136, 138, 143, 154, 159, 165, 183, 189, 196, 205, 210, 212
Historia Foto: p.53, 54
Huber/Fantuz Olimpio: p.23
Huber/R. Schmid: p.3 (right below), 75, 119 (right below), 175
IFA Bilderteam: p.119 (right above)

laif/Dreysse: p.174
laif/Modrow: p.111 (right above), 163
laif/Piepenburg: p.6, 10, 121, 155, 169, 214
laif/Tophoven: p.8/9, 12 (below), 18, 68
laif/Zanettini: front cover inside, p.4 (right below), 5 (left below), 13, 29, 86, 107 (left above), 146, 148, 168, 173, 186, 203
Look/Friedel: p.97
Look/B. Müller: p.20
Look/J. Richter: p.11 (centre, below), 14, 21 (left above), 33, 98, 104/105, 192, 206
Schapowalow: p.115 (left below)
Storto: p.5 (right below)
White Star/M. Gumm: p.11 (above), 12 (centre), 22, 58/59, 67, 76, 84, 106, 107 (below), 113 (right above and below), 125, 181, 182, 194, 201, 209, back cover outside

Cover photo: digital Vision
back cover outside: White Star/M. Gumm

PUBLISHER'S INFORMATION

Illustrations etc: 125 illustrations, 20 maps and diagrams, one large island map
Text: Birgit Borowski
Achim Bourmer (Baedeker Specials)
Hans Jürgen Fründt (Etiquette)
Editing: Baedeker editorial team (John Sykes)
Translation: Barbara Schmidt-Runkel
Cartography: Christoph Gallus, Hohberg; MAIRDUMONT/Falk Verlag, Ostfildern (island map)
3D illustrations: jangled nerves, Stuttgart
Design: independent Medien-Design, Munich; Kathrin Schemel

Editor-in-chief: Rainer Eisenschmid, Baedeker Ostfildern

1st edition 2009

Based on Baedeker Allianz Reiseführer »Gran Canaria«

Copyright: Karl Baedeker Verlag, Ostfildern
Publication rights: MAIRDUMONT GmbH & Co; Ostfildern

Printed in China